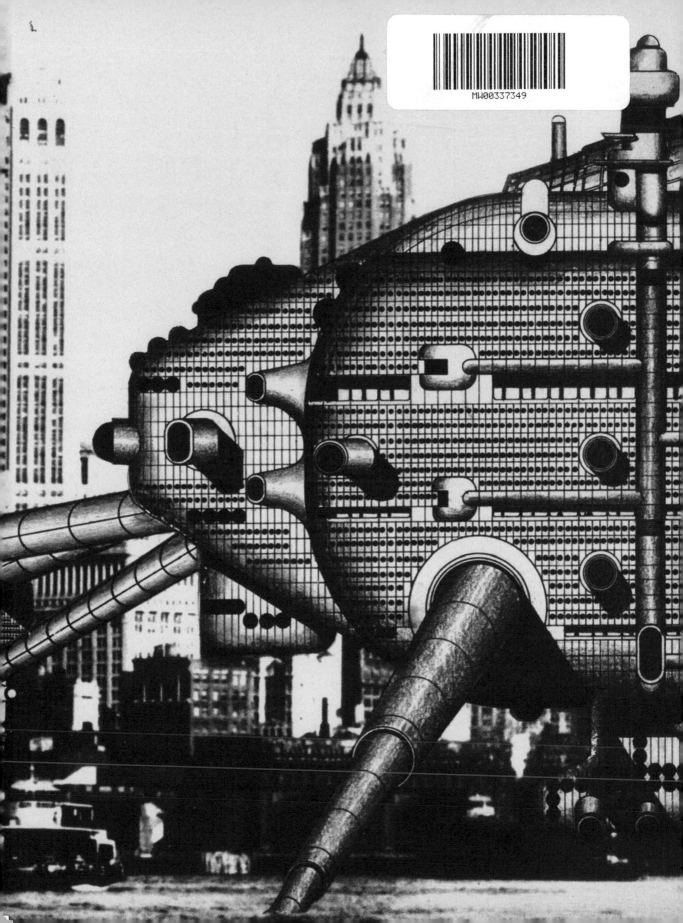

PHANTOM
ARCHITECTURE

PHANTOM ARCHITECTURE

PHILIP WILKINSON

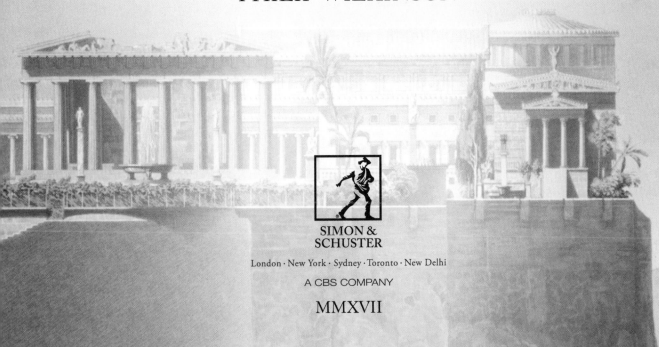

SIMON &
SCHUSTER

London · New York · Sydney · Toronto · New Delhi

A CBS COMPANY

MMXVII

To Zoë

Н. ПУНИН

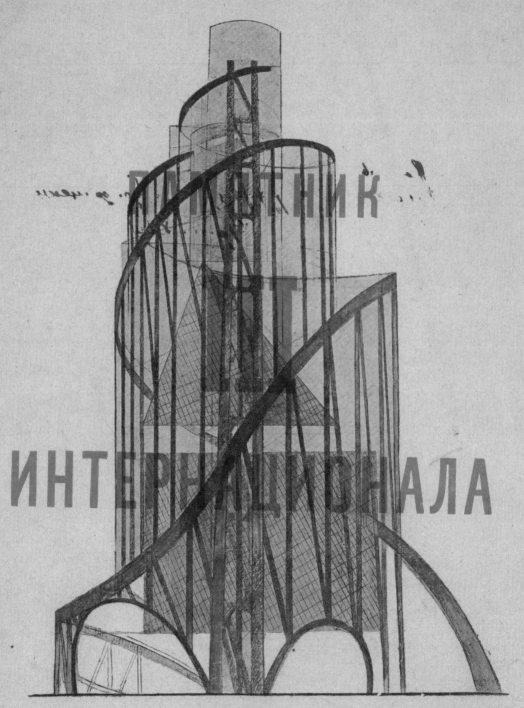

ПАМЯТНИК

III

ИНТЕРНАЦИОНАЛА

Проект худ. В. Е. ТАТЛИНА

ПЕТЕРБУРГ

Издание Отдела Изобразительных Искусств Н. К. П.

1920 г.

CONTENTS

INTRODUCTION

A vast dome covering most of Midtown Manhattan, a royal palace right next to the Parthenon in Athens, a skyscraper 1 mile (1.6km) high, a triumphal arch in the shape of an elephant: some of the most exciting buildings in the history of architecture were never constructed. These are the designs in which architects pushed materials to the limits, explored challenging new ideas, defied convention, indulged creative whims or pointed the way towards the future. This book tells the story of fifty of these buildings and shows how, although they exist only as plans, drawings or models, they still fascinate people today, living a ghostly life as phantom architecture.

There are many reasons why designs stay on the drawing board. The builder can run out of money, hit unexpected structural difficulties or fall foul of regulations. Architects can clash with clients, lose out to rivals, change their minds, produce a design that is judged wrong for the site or unfit for its purpose or is said to be 'too far head of its time'.

The plans survive, though, as fascinating and sometimes breathtaking evidence of what might have been. Many were unlucky masterpieces. Sir Christopher Wren's 'Great Model' design for St Paul's Cathedral would have been a great building and a centrepiece for London. It fell by the wayside because it was not traditional enough for London's clergy. Mies van der Rohe's Berlin Friedrichstrasse Tower and Eliel Saarinen's design for the Chicago Tribune skyscraper – both runners-up in architectural competitions – were masterpieces that showcased new kinds of tall building. In one sense, these plans were failures, because they were never built, but they were hugely successful, in the sense that their visionary designs stayed in people's minds, and were studied and imitated by architects all over the world.

Some of the most outstanding architectural designs ever created have this phantom life. Among the most remarkable works of the French eighteenth-century architect Étienne-Louis Boullée, for example, were designs for a French national library and an enormous spherical monument to the scientist Isaac Newton. Neither was built, but their drawings live on because of their striking and pure architectural form, because they sum up visually and spatially the great intellectual movement known as the Enlightenment and because they survive in engravings of such surpassing beauty. Boullée's buildings were so vast and impractical that they stood little chance of getting off the drawing board, but their qualities give the designs enduring fascination.

Boullée dreamed of gigantic buildings, but some people wanted to transform entire towns or to build from scratch ideal cities or utopias. The notion of creating the perfect place goes back to the ancient world, to the Republic of the Greek philosopher Plato, who was more interested in society and government than in architecture. Philosophers and artists of the Renaissance followed in his footsteps, and sometimes gave visual form to their ideas, making plans of ideal cities or haunting images of their buildings.

Renaissance ideal city plans usually took perfect geometrical form – a circle or a square enclosed by a wall, with streets radiating like the spokes of a wheel or making concentric circles. Designs such as these were a reaction against the unplanned chaos of medieval cities, with their narrow, twisting alleys, and strove to impose architectural order which, it was hoped, would reflect and contain ordered government and society. There were also attempts to solve practical problems with city planning, such as Leonardo da Vinci's Split-Level City, proposed as a way of reducing the spread of infectious disease.

Schemes for rebuilding existing towns or cities such as Urbino or Milan had little chance of coming to fruition, even in the prosperous Renaissance period – the cost and upheaval would have been too great. Twentieth-century proposals to rebuild swathes of Paris or Barcelona would have caused still greater disruption and needed an even bigger budget. However, twentieth-century ideal cities such as Le Corbusier's Ville Radieuse proved hugely influential, especially in Europe when rebuilding took place after the Second World War. Few cities, though, got designs that were as thoroughly thought through as Le Corbusier's. His successors built Corbusian tower blocks, but were not allowed enough green apace around them; they copied the visual style of his Unités d'habitation (buildings containing shops, childcare facilities and restaurants, as well as flats) but built apartment blocks not communities.

If some of these plans look like impossible dreams, this was not usually how they began. Architects are often confronted with crises that require quick and ingenious solutions. The spread of bubonic plague in Renaissance Europe, the unprecedented growth of nineteenth-century cities, reconstruction after the devastating damage caused by the Second World War – all of these sent artists, planners and architects in search of designs that were worthy of pressing needs. The responses can be as unexpected as the challenges that brought them into being. When faced with the gridlock caused in Victorian London by the city's rapid expansion, engineer Joseph Paxton came up with the Great Victorian Way, a combination of covered shopping street, housing development and two-level railway on a gigantic scale – the structure would have made an 11 mile (17.7km) loop around the centre of the city. Paxton saw this structure mainly as a practical solution to a real need, but in designing something so huge he had also created a symbol of London's success and importance.

Some architecture – triumphal arches or national monuments, for example – is meant to be mainly symbolic. Symbolism of something with large claims to power or significance, such as absolute monarchy in eighteenth-century France or communism in post-revolutionary Russia, can lead to structures that look ungainly or grandiose. A French architect, Charles-François Ribart, conceived a building in the shape of an elephant as a monument to King Louis XV, which is an absurd idea but charming and interesting historically. It is all the more remarkable when seen in terms of its proposed site – right on the Champs Élyseés in Paris. Russian sculptor Vladimir Tatlin's huge, spiral-shaped Monument to the Third International also had a provocative site, against a backdrop of eighteenth-century St Petersburg (known as Petrograd when the tower was designed). This structure, all iron struts and braces and glass boxes, is odd in a very different way from Ribart's elephant. It had a major influence on later sculpture and visual arts, even though all that ever existed of it was some artwork and a few models.

One reason unbuilt designs survive is the sheer quality of the drawings. From the rapid Expressionist pencil sketches of Erich Mendelsohn to the beautifully composed coloured paintings of Zaha Hadid, these works are a feast for the eye. So, unlike the precise, hard-edged technical drawings of some designers, they force us to look closely before they reveal their secrets. Some are more literal, but just as beguiling. Frank Lloyd Wright's vast drawing of his 1 mile- (1.6km-)

high skyscraper for Chicago or Karl Friedrich Schinkel's elegant coloured illustrations of his proposed royal palace on the Acropolis in Athens are so persuasive they almost make us accept buildings that are in many ways unthinkable. For most people of the twenty-first century, the idea of building a nineteenth-century palace right next to the Parthenon or a 1 mile- (1.6km-) high monster dwarfing the tall towers of the windy city feels just wrong, but the drawings are so good that you almost give way to unreason.

There are lots of other reasons for remembering the phantom buildings in this book. Some are the rich fruit of individual endeavour, some are key steps in an architect's development, some are highly influential on other architects, some are just charming examples of the eccentric and the odd. Most are important because of where they point. A famous, or notorious, example comes from the 1960s, when the engineer and inventor Richard Buckminster Fuller came up with the most bizarre of his many odd ideas – to construct an enormous dome over most of midtown Manhattan. Enclosing an enormous area of New York City like this would have, Fuller argued, great benefits for energy consumption and water use. Applied elsewhere, vast domes might enable us to build cities in inhospitable parts of the globe. Fuller knew that he had no chance of constructing a dome over New York. But he thought it worthwhile to propose the idea because of where it might lead – to lighter, more energy-efficient structures and cities, decades before such issues had the urgency they do now.

So the buildings in this book are interesting for all kinds of reasons. They are the cherished schemes of rulers or city governments; attempts by architects and planners to show us better ways to live; buildings that glorify heroes or leaders; responses to urgent and pressing needs; endeavours to turn architectural norms upside-down. They all deserve our attention.

CHAPTER 1
IDEAL WORLDS

What would the ideal city be like? How would you

Throughout the Middle Ages and the Renaissance period, people strove to answer these questions in a variety of ways. In the Middle Ages, the answer was usually based on religion – a perfect cathedral as the image of heaven on Earth or a monastery as an ideal Christian community. Later, during the Renaissance, it was more likely to take the form of an ideal city designed using the Classical proportions of ancient Greek or Roman architecture to create buildings, streets and piazzas of surpassing elegance. As they were ideals, these places were never likely to be built – it would have been both expensive and impractical to construct new cities for the people of Milan or Urbino and to relocate every house, business, palace and church. But the plans remained something to aspire to when a street or piazza was redeveloped, or a major building was reconstructed.

house the perfect community?

The people who imagined these ideals and put them down on paper were usually not architects as we understand the term today. The profession of architect, in the sense of a person who trained to become a specialist designer of buildings, evolved gradually, during the fifteenth and sixteenth centuries, and those who designed buildings and towns before this time combined the role of designer with that of master mason or sculptor, craftsman, engineer, painter or writer. It was most probably a monk who drew up the plan of the ideal monastery of St Gall, Switzerland, in the ninth century. The person who created the most beautiful ideal city design for the Duke of Urbino in the 1480s was a painter. Leonardo da Vinci, creator of a famous ideal city design for the Duke of Milan a few years later, mastered every skill from oil painting to engineering.

Coming from such different places and periods, these ideal worlds varied hugely in appearance and style, ranging from the austere simplicity of medieval monasteries to the princely magnificence of some Renaissance designs. The traces their creators left behind – the half-built fabric of Beauvais Cathedral, the stunning Urbino painting, the complex and detailed plan of St Gall, Leonardo's fascinating sketches, the city plans of Sforzinda and Christianopolis – recall vanished times and ideals, and haunt the minds of anyone who has seen them.

THE ABBEY OF ST GALL

*c.*820

An Ideal Benedictine Monastery

Nasty, brutish and short: that is how we are used to thinking of life a thousand years ago. For most, there was no formal education, work began in childhood and was grindingly hard, and home was a draughty hovel with no running water, no artificial light and no sanitation; healthcare was minimal and crude. For one group, though, things could be different. Monks and nuns worked hard and prayed hard, but did so in surprisingly sophisticated surroundings. Monasteries might have been cold and spartan by modern standards, but many had clean running water, decent lavatories and the best healthcare available. Monks could read and write, and did so by candlelight. By the standards of the time, they lived in decent conditions.

One astonishing ninth-century manuscript shows what the ideal monastery might have been like. It is an enormous document, 44 × 30in (112 × 77.5cm), on five pieces of parchment, meticulously stitched together. On it is the ground plan of a large and well-equipped Benedictine monastery. It shows the church and all the ancillary buildings – dormitories, workshops, kitchens, infirmary, stables and so on – necessary to support a self-contained community of up to 110 monks, more than a hundred workers and their guests.

This document is known as the St Gall plan, after the abbey of St Gall (now St Gallen) in Switzerland, where it is kept. It is the only surviving major architectural drawing from the period between the fall of Rome in the fifth century AD and *c.*1250. The scribe who drew it seems to have thought of everything: dedicated buildings for every aspect of the abbey's farm, for example, and workshops for specialists such as a wood turner and barrel maker. Short annotations on the plan identify these buildings, and areas such as a garden and an orchard. Looking closer, we can see how carefully they have been considered. Everything is arranged in ordered rows. The abbot's house is linked by a passage to the church. The servants' quarters are conveniently near the workshops and farm buildings, and well away from the abbot's house. Some parts of the monastery even have underfloor heating, similar to the hypocausts used by the

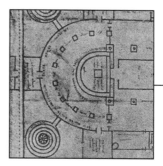

The church of St Gall is shown on the plan with apsidal (rounded) ends. The western end has a square entrance porch in the centre and is flanked by a pair of circular towers.

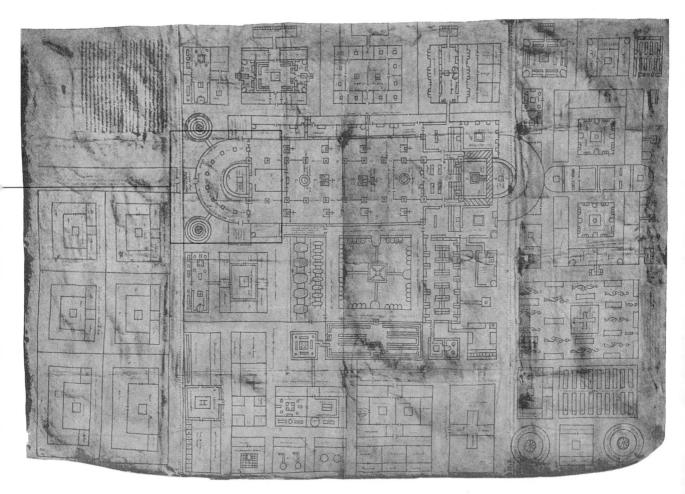

Romans, and there are plenty of lavatories, sited near the edge of the site to aid waste disposal.

The plan was drawn up in Austria, at the monastery of Reichenau, and was sent by Reichenau's abbot to Gozbertus, the abbot of St Gall between 816 and 836, who was planning to rebuild his monastery. As far as is known, the document has remained at St Gall ever since. However, the extensive buildings it depicts would not have fitted the site at St Gall, and scholars believe that it is actually an ideal plan, showing the monastery that both men would have liked to have built, had they had the perfect site and access to enough materials and labour. The parchment bears a dedication to Abbot Gozbertus, and this hints that the plan is for meditation and study rather than a precise blueprint for his new buildings: 'For thee, my sweetest son Gozbertus, have I drawn this briefly annotated copy of the layout of the monastic buildings, with which you may exercise your ingenuity and recognize my devotion.'

The large parchment plan includes some forty structures arranged around the church and its adjoining cloister. Each structure, from infirmary to brew house, is identified with its own label.

As he began his building project, Gozbertus might have contemplated the plan and tried to incorporate as many of the details of it as he could. In the event, his rebuilding was confined mostly to the abbey's church, which in turn was replaced in the seventeenth century. Although his buildings do not survive, archaeological evidence has shown that Gozbertus's church was different in dimensions and design from the one on the plan, confirming that he did not use it as a literal model.

The St Gall plan is exemplary both in the sense that it has every facility and that it embodies the latest monastic ideas – the reforms that the church was introducing at the time,

This 1982 perspective drawing by Ernest Born shows how the interior of the church might have appeared. The view shows the nave, looking towards the tomb of St Gall at the east end of the church.

such as providing accommodation for lay workers inside the monastic complex rather than outside. It is a highly ordered plan, and this order is no doubt meant to reflect the order of the Benedictine rule, by which the monks lived. The document represents the ideal version of a very idealistic way of life.

The abbots of most small medieval monasteries would have found the facilities in the plan very lavish. For example, it was usual for monasteries to have dedicated accommodation for the novices (the young monks still in 'training' before taking their full vows) and for the sick; in the St Gall plan, both novices and the infirm have their own separate complexes, each with its own cloister, church, refectory and dormitory. Everything else, from the guest accommodation to the profusion of workshops, is on a large scale.

Architectural historians such as Ernest Born have published drawings showing what the monastery might have looked like had it been built. The style is the Romanesque of the period, with thick stone walls, small windows, semicircular arches, and round towers with conical roofs. The interiors would have been very plain, but the church would have had columns in the style of the period, perhaps topped with capitals decorated with carved foliage.

Medieval monks devoted themselves to God's service, spent much of their time in prayer, liturgy or work, took vows of poverty, chastity and obedience, and lived mostly within the walled confines of the monastic enclave. Their lives were always those of ideals, and monks strove (in theory at least and often in practice) to live as close to these goals as they could. The plan of St Gall is an architectural picture of these ideals, with every conceivable building provided. It is not surprising that, in the real world, limits of money, space and willpower meant that the plan was never carried out in full.

But in the twenty-first century it might be built, not in Switzerland but in Messkirch, Baden-Württemberg, in southwestern Germany. Here Campus Galli is an ongoing project to build a monastery following the St Gall plan, using the materials and techniques that were available in the ninth century. It is a long-term project, and relies on raising income from tourists who visit the site. It is also a fascinating piece of experimental archaeology, exploring medieval building techniques and telling participants much about the difficulties faced by their ancient predecessors. Finally, it is a tribute to the lasting power of the St Gall plan.

BEAUVAIS CATHEDRAL NAVE

1225

The Ultimate Medieval Cathedral

The thirteenth century saw a kind of race among French bishops to build the most magnificent and highest cathedral. The motivation was religious. Medieval clergy saw churches as images of heaven on Earth. The bishops wanted their cathedrals to reach closer and closer to the heavens and they demanded ever-larger stained-glass windows, to fill their interiors with heavenly light. The great cathedral of Nôtre Dame in Paris, built between 1163 and 1250, set the standard, with an interior more than 112ft (34m) high. There followed a clutch of cathedrals – Chartres, Bourges and Reims – with heights around 121ft (37m) and Amiens, with its staggering 139ft (42.3m) nave. One man, Milo of Nanteuil, Bishop of Beauvais, wanted to build even higher and create a cathedral still more daring and dizzying than Amiens – 156ft (47.5m) was his target.

Building this high was always going to be a challenge, especially because of the great weight of the heavy stone vault that forms the ceiling of a medieval cathedral. When you combine a stone vault with big windows, there is not much wall left to hold up the vault, and the weight of stone tends to push the walls outwards, making them collapse. Gothic architecture provided the answer, because it used flying buttresses – large, arch-like structures – to support the building from the outside. Flying buttresses push the vault inwards and take the stresses and strains down to ground level, relieving the pressure on the walls and allowing larger windows. So a Gothic cathedral had a stone skeleton of flying buttresses and pointed arches that held the whole building together. This kind of construction meant that Beauvais could become the tallest of all the Gothic cathedrals.

Milo's rebuilding project began in 1225, when the old cathedral at Beauvais was damaged in a fire. Fire was a frequent hazard in medieval cities with their wooden buildings, and this was not the first blaze to affect the cathedral. But this time the damage was severe and Milo decided to build a replacement. The east end of the damaged

The view looking up towards the stone-vaulted ceiling of the completed choir of Beauvais Cathedral shows a space of vertiginous height, bathed in light.

cathedral was therefore demolished, leaving part of the nave to function as a place of worship in the early phases of the building work.

Work began on the new cathedral soon after the fire. By 1272, the cathedral choir – its eastern arm – was completed. At some point during the construction, the clergy and masons took the decision to make this the highest vaulted space in Europe. If this was not daring enough, the masons of Beauvais also made the choir's supporting masonry very slender, to allow for larger-than-ever windows. The result was a precarious structure which, shimmering with stained glass and extending ever upwards, must have amazed contemporaries, who had never seen a space so vast or so high. It was an architectural triumph.

But the triumph was short-lived. In 1284, just twelve years after the completion of the choir vault, part of it collapsed, perhaps because its buttresses were not able to withstand storm-force winds. A rebuilding campaign began almost immediately, and the vault was reinforced with extra ribs and supports. However, a turning point had been reached. The cathedrals built in the next 200 years were all on a smaller scale and, although this might have had something to do with the financial restrictions imposed by major events such as the Hundred Years' War, the collapse at Beauvais must have made builders pause. No other medieval mason tried to beat the height record set by the choir of Beauvais Cathedral.

But only the choir was competed in the thirteenth century. It stood alone until the sixteenth century, when a new building project was launched, to construct the transept and central tower, the intended second or middle phase of the building. The transept maintained the same height as the choir, and the tower was set to be even higher – a monster of some 500ft (153m) was begun, but this too collapsed. The masons tidied up the debris and drew a line under the work by finishing off the transept. The cathedral still lacked a nave (its western arm), but this was never built. The masons inserted a west wall to make the building weatherproof, and the church remained in its half-finished state.

The missing nave would have virtually doubled the length of the building, to the same vaulting height, creating the most awe-inspiring vistas of any medieval church. It would also have helped balance the cathedral both visually and structurally. As it is, the building has been fragile ever since it was begun. At some time, perhaps soon after the first vault collapse in 1284,

Much of the masonry of the cathedral, seen here in cross-section, is in the massive buttresses that support the cathedral from the outside. Wooden-framed roofs above the stone vaults add to the building's great height.

iron tie rods were inserted to help make the building stronger. At one point in the nineteenth century, the rods were removed and the building began to vibrate dangerously in high winds. They were quickly replaced with steel bars.

Medieval masons had enormous experience of structures, built up over centuries – especially the twelfth and thirteenth centuries when they constructed the most daring vaulted cathedrals. Partly by trial and error, partly by calculation, they accumulated knowledge of the best angle and curve for a flying buttress, the weight and size of the ribs of a vault. They knew to within quite small tolerances how thin they could make their walls, and how slender their piers. But they were always trying to push that bit harder, to get a few feet more height, or accommodate a few square feet more stained glass. Building collapses were not uncommon, and the one at Beauvais showed them the limits of what you could build with finely balanced stone. Today, the cathedral, its walls cracked, its structure held together with tie rods of steel, and its transept propped with trusses of wood and metal, is still a triumph – one that eloquently demonstrates equally the daring and the fragility of Gothic architecture.

SFORZINDA

Antonio di Pietro Averlino, c.1450

A City in Which to Recreate the Golden Age

People often long for the 'good old days', the mythical time in the distant past when everyone was innocent and honest, when kings and governments ruled justly and without corruption, when humans and animals lived in harmony, when no one was poor, everyone was happy and the sun always shone. This ideal world can take many forms, from the Garden of Eden to some historical period when life was allegedly better and fairer. The ancient Greeks and Romans had a myth of the Golden Age, a period at the beginning of time when, as the Greek poet Hesiod puts it: 'Men lived like gods without sorrow of heart.'

When they rediscovered the culture of the ancient world, the writers and artists of the Italian Renaissance also rediscovered the Golden Age. Renaissance Italians lived in city states such as Florence and Siena, places of great prosperity and culture, but also not immune from mishap, corruption, disease and war. They surrounded themselves with beautiful works of art, but such beauty did not always go hand in hand with a well-run life. One way the Renaissance Italians hoped to recreate the mythical happy age – or at least to get closer to its happiness – was to plan ideal cities, in which beautiful architecture reflected fair and just government.

One of the most successful cities in Italy in the second half of the fifteenth century was Milan. From 1450, it was ruled by the Sforza family, a dynasty founded by Francesco Sforza, who had conquered the city that year and became its fourth duke. His principal architect and engineer was a man called Antonio di Pietro Averlino, usually known as Filarete (lover of excellence). Filarete was born in Florence but came to work for Francesco in Milan at the beginning of his reign, building the city's Ospedale Maggiore and working on the reconstruction of Francesco's castle. Filarete was also a writer, who produced a long book on architecture, part of which is a description of an ideal city, called Sforzinda in honour of the duke.

Filarete's description of Sforzinda takes the form of a detailed account of the city and a fictionalized narrative explaining its origins. The architect describes the city's layout,

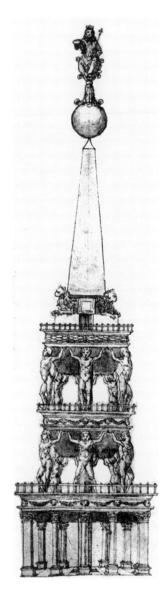

ABOVE *This obelisk, supported by carved stone figures, shows the ornate style of Filarete's designs.*

OPPOSITE *Filarete's manuscript is illustrated with line drawings of the main structures and architectural details.*

prinpiare pohe furono tante lepietre diqueste ruine chetutti isondamenti dun
partita cioe della croce della parte degluomini furono fatti fino alpian tereno

Siche essendo disegnato illuogho doue far sidoueua questo spedale alnome di
Cristo & della anuntiata fu ordinata una solenne procassione collo arcue
scouo & contutta lachiericia Elduha Francesco sforza insieme colla illustrissi
ma bianchba Maria Ilconte Galeazzo & madonna Ipolita & Filippo maria
& altri suoi figliuoli cumpiu altri Signori intraquali uifu ilsignore Marche
se di Mantoua el Signore Guglielmo dimon ferrato fuui ancora due inbosca
dori del Re alfonso di Ragona Ilnome deluno fu ilconte di Santo angelo
laltro fu uno gentile huomo napoletano fuui ancora il Signore Taddeo da Im
la & piu & piu huomini degni iquali colpopolo di Milano uennono colla detta
procassione alluogho diputato & disegnato doue chelaprima pietra sidoueua
collocare & gunti alluogho predeto io insieme con uno diquegli diputati fu po
ta lapietra laquale era statuita adouere mettere nelfondamento sopra laqua
le era scripto ilmillesimo & ancora ildi elmese ilquale millesimo correua 1457
adi 4 daprile & cosi certe altre cirimonie lequali erano queste cioe prima fu
tre uasi diuetro Uno pieno dacqua laltro di uino laltro dolio & Io ghordinai
uno uaso diterra nelquale era una cassetta dipionbo doue era piu cose intra
laltre uera certe memorie diteste scolpite di alcuni huomini degni difama &
apresentare queste cose doue lacima era fatta adouerla mettere & ini cantato
certo busiao el Signore insieme colpontefice & io insieme colloro collocamo que
sta pietra collaltre sopradette cose pdare inquesto luogho una dimostratione alle
psone glisu fatto come adire uno segno o uuoi dire termine glisu fatto come
adire una colomna o uuoi dire uno pilastro nelquale fu scripto uno pigramo
fatto p messer Tommaxo darieti & diceua inquesta forma cioe:

FRANCISCVS · SFORTIA · DVX · IIII · SED · Q VIAMISSVM · PER · P PRAECESSO
RVM: OBITVM · VRBIS · IMPERIVM · RECVPERAVIT · HOC · MVNVS · CRISTI
PAVPERIBVS · DEDIT · FVNDAVIT · Q VE · M CCCC LVII · DIE · P XII · APRILIS

Siche tutte queste cose uolle chefussono dipinte nelportico & comemorate fane pri
mo dibuoni maestri imodo era degnia cosa auedere Era ancora sopra alla po
ta delmezzo uno pigramo fatto plodegnio poheta philelfo come dinanzi e scrip
to & diceua /cosi uolle questo nostro Signore chesidipigniessi inquesto della nostra
nuoua citta & cosi umanzi alla porta fu fatto uno diquesti termini maquesto
fu fatto d'bellissimo marmo & fu scolpito intorno didegne cose intralaltre glisu
scolpito la immagine delsignore Come egli misse & colloco laprima pietra &ca
cora lamia & alcune altre degne memorie Et disopra nella sommita uno be
llo fiorimento colla immagine della annunptiata Disopra uera scolpito ancora
iquanro tempi dellano & tutto ledisitio come sifaceua & piu gentilezze lequa
li dilenedra credo glipiacera come piace adni uede quello dimilano Siche for
mto questo spedale ilquale allui somamente piacque Et intrallaltre cose de
ome quando alcuno forestiere lauesse uicitato facena uedere questo p uno de
degni hedifitij chenella terra sua fusse:

which is based on an eight-pointed star formed by overlaying two squares, the whole surrounded by a circular moat. He gives each of the eight points of the star a defensive tower, and each of the star's inner angles a gateway. The gateways open onto straight main streets leading to the centre of the city, like the spokes of a wheel. At the very centre of the city is a large square, which has a public water supply and also contains a tall tower, for which Filarete includes quite a detailed drawing.

The architect also provides detailed depictions or accounts of key buildings such as the cathedral and ducal palace, schools (separate ones for boys and girls) and an extraordinary building called the House of Vice and Virtue, which has a brothel on the lower floors and an academy higher up. Trade and commerce brought real Renaissance cities their prosperity, so this function is catered for in Sforzinda too. Each of the main streets has a square at its mid-point, and each of these squares houses a market. The city also has canals, linking to a river, so that goods could be brought in and out with ease.

To explain the origins of the city and its roots in the Golden Age, Filarete gives Sforzinda a fictional ancestor. His story of Sforzinda's construction describes how, when the foundations were being dug for one of the buildings, the workers unearthed a box made of stone. In the box was a book, called the Golden Book, written by a king, Zogalia, who long ago had been ruler of a city called Plusiapolis. In the book Zogalia writes how he

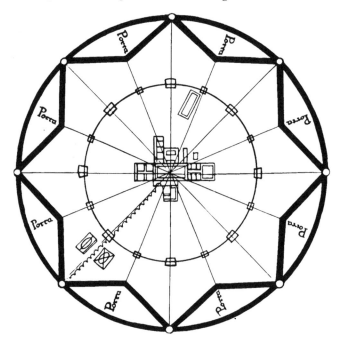

Star-shaped plans such as Sforzinda's were not unusual in city plans in the Renaissance period. They were effective both architecturally and in terms of fortification.

believes that his own kingdom will fall to barbarians and that Plusiapolis will vanish. So he has written the book in order that future people will know something about the lost city, and benefit from knowledge of it and its architecture. One of the buildings is a temple, which Filarete makes the basis for the Cathedral of Sforzinda, linking Zogalia and his architect with Francesco Sforza and Filarete.

By pretending that his ideal city is actually a copy of an earlier ideal city – and by calling the book discovered in the stone box the Golden Book – Filarete makes a clear connection between Sforzinda and the mythical Golden Age. He is implying that Duke Francesco could recreate the Golden Age by building an ideal city and honouring it with his wise government. As well as offering a fresh and interesting city plan, therefore, Filarete is also complimenting his lord – always a wise thing for an artist to do in the Renaissance, when every artist needed a patron.

Francesco would also have recognized other symbolic references in the plan. The number eight (the eight-pointed star and the eight radiating streets) is clearly very important in the design, and the eight points are produced by drawing two overlapping squares, implying two groups of four. This is probably an allusion to the four primary elements (earth, air, fire and water) and four basic qualities (hot, cold, dry and wet) laid down by Aristotle. These groups are repeated widely in ancient and Renaissance writings and were seen to be fundamental to life – everything in the universe being made of the four elements and being understandable in terms of the four qualities. The kinds of scientific writing that Francesco would have admired – treatises on astrology, astronomy and alchemy – all explained the universe in these terms.

Astrology was especially important to Filarete and his patron. Filarete's book has the court astrologer telling his patron the most propitious times for laying the foundation stone of the city. The date he comes up with is 15 April 1460 at 10.20am, which, as the scholar Berthold Hub has pointed out, is the precise moment at which the sun enters the first sign of the zodiac, Aries – in many traditions the planetary situation at the time God created the world. Filarete's ideal city is a new start, but looks back to the first beginning, linking Filarete and his patron Francesco Sforza with the most exalted creator of all.

IDEAL CITY

Francesco di Giorgio Martini (attrib.), *c*.1480

The Ideal City of the Renaissance

When the artists and writers of the Renaissance rediscovered the Classical civilization of ancient Rome, the culture of Europe was transformed. The art of Piero della Francesca and Sandro Botticelli, the sculpture of Donatello and the scientific discoveries and inventions of Leonardo da Vinci were all made possible. There was a revolution in building, too, with the pointed arches of Gothic architecture being replaced by the Classical style of the Renaissance. But these changes took place in crowded, chaotic, medieval towns with narrow, winding streets and buildings that had grown organically over the centuries. Having rediscovered the art and architecture of ancient Rome, people hoped to reconstruct their towns in Rome's image, with buildings in the Classical style arranged harmoniously and also equipped

with the best the age could offer in modern facilities, from academies to aqueducts.

What would the perfect fifteenth-century city look like, if you could start from scratch? Three of the most haunting and beautiful images of the Renaissance offer an answer. They depict ideal cities and are among the most enigmatic paintings of the period: a trio of depictions of imaginary city squares, painted on wooden panels in elongated landscape format in the 1480s. No one is sure who painted them, or where the panels were originally located, or even what their precise purpose was – they may have been attached to the walls of a room as part of the interior decoration, but they could equally have been incorporated into pieces of furniture.

The panels seem to belong together but are now held in museums in Baltimore, USA and Berlin, and in the Ducal Palace at Urbino, where they may all have originated. They date to Urbino's heyday under its most celebrated duke, Federico da Montefeltro, a military leader and patron of artists and scholars who was lord of Urbino from 1444 to 1482. Federico had many artistic interests – architecture and city planning among them.

Of the three related Ideal City panel paintings, the one at Urbino is the most striking. The subtle variations in masonry tones, the harmonious forms of the Classical buildings and the geometrically patterned pavement together create an impression that combines balance with variety.

In his *studiolo* (the private room in which he entertained only his closest friends and associates), the walls are decorated with stunning inlaid wooden panels, some of which illustrate architectural subjects. Federico would have been an enthusiastic viewer of the painted panels, too. Another likely link to Federico is the triumphal arch that occupies the centre of the Baltimore panel, alluding to his famous military victories.

These ideal city paintings have been attributed to several artists, including Piero della Francesca, but a strong candidate is Francesco di Giorgio Martini, an architect and artist who worked for Federico as a designer of fortifications. Martini was a practical military architect who pioneered the idea of building fortresses on a star-shaped plan with triangular bastions – a form of fortification that was highly effective and much used in the sixteenth and seventeenth centuries. In addition, he was an architectural theorist and author of a book, *Trattato di architettura, ingegneria e arte militaria* (Treatise on Architecture, Engineering and Military Arts), which contains the plans of several ideal fortresses and cities. Among these plans are various polygonal city layouts, including a striking octagonal one, designed for a site on a hill, with a main street that ascends the slope in the form of a spiral.

All of these plans are designed with symmetry and harmony in mind, and the images in the panel paintings are also very harmoniously arranged. The buildings on either side of the piazzas are Classical and symmetrical in their proportions, although the sides of the squares are not mirror images of one another – these are ordered spaces but not regimented ones. At the centre of the square in the Urbino panel is a circular church (a temple, as it would have been described in the Renaissance, in deference to its ancient Classical origins). The circle was an image of perfection in the Middle Ages and Renaissance – the planets move in circles, and the circle is the purest geometrical shape, with every point on its circumference equidistant from the centre. The door of this building is open, indicating that one is welcome to enter the perfect space within.

The paintings show purely urban spaces, very much built environments, without visible trees or gardens. But in the distance in the Urbino panel a couple of slivers of green landscape are just visible. This hint of the countryside outside the city suggests that it is hilly, indicating, if the panel was indeed made for the ducal palace, that the setting could be Urbino itself. It suggests, in other words, that Federico's own city could partake of this perfection.

One of the striking things about the designs is their sense of space. This is partly because they are almost empty of people – only the Baltimore panel includes any figures, and art historians think that these may well have been added after the painting was completed; the Berlin painting shows ships in a harbour beyond the square. This emptiness gives the cities an atmosphere of silence but also hints at the perfection of these places – even humanity, with all its faults and troubles, is absent.

The sense of space around the buildings is in dramatic contrast to most fifteenth-century cities, with their narrow streets and their lack of space between the buildings. The Renaissance dukes and their artistic employees wanted generous civic spaces, where people could meet, talk and do business, and, for all their lack of people, Martini's paintings would have reminded Federico of this social role of the city.

No Renaissance ruler quite achieved the sense of order portrayed in Martini's paintings. Cities such as Florence, Siena and Ferrara come close, with their elegant squares and monumental palaces, but a real city redevelopment is usually a compromise with an ancient street plan or old buildings that cannot be demolished. Few city builders have the opportunity to make a completely new start. Enigmatic and haunting, the paintings of Martini show what the architects of the Renaissance could have done if they had had the chance.

The Baltimore painting, with its diverse architectural forms, has been attributed to the architect and artist Fra Carnevale as well as to Martini.

MILAN, ITALY

SPLIT-LEVEL CITY

Leonardo da Vinci, *c.*1490

Leonardo's Solution to the Spread of Bubonic Plague

For centuries, plague was a disaster that recurred across Europe. The devastating outbreak of the Black Death in 1348–50 is the most famous example, killing perhaps half of Europe's population, but there were many other epidemics. One particularly bad one was in Milan in the 1480s. It cut swathes through the population. Rich people, including its ruler, Lodovico Sforza il Moro, left the city. Lodovico would not even open letters from home unless servants had decontaminated them using strong perfumes.

One of the people who made the perfumes thought to remove the taint of plague might have been Leonardo da Vinci. The artist, engineer and inventor worked for Lodovico from *c.*1482 to 1499 and was famous for being able to turn his hand to any problem – artistic or scientific. He did some of his greatest work in Milan, painting two masterpieces – *The Virgin of the Rocks* and *The Last Supper* – and compiling notebooks packed with inventions, ideas and designs that sum up the diversity of his genius. One result of the plague was that Leonardo began to focus increasingly on architecture and town planning, in the hope that he could design a city where the disease was less likely to spread. He was already interested in architecture, and this interest must have been stimulated by contact with the great Renaissance architect Donato Bramante, who also worked for Lodovico. Looking at the question of city planning, though, was more than an architectural problem for Leonardo as it also drew on his expertise as a scientist and engineer.

In the fifteenth century, scientific understanding of infectious diseases was primitive. No one knew how they were caused; the bacteria that carried them had not been discovered. People thought infectious diseases were spread through the air by scent. Decaying matter, whether animal faeces, rotting vegetables or infected flesh, smells bad; people thought that the smell came from a miasma – a poisonous vapour made up of tiny bits of decaying material that travelled through the air, carrying the infection with it. Leonardo supposed that crowded late-medieval cities encouraged miasma to form, making them

Leonardo's drawings of churches show his deep interest in architecture. These designs have round elements such as domes and towers – the circle was a widely recognized symbol of perfection.

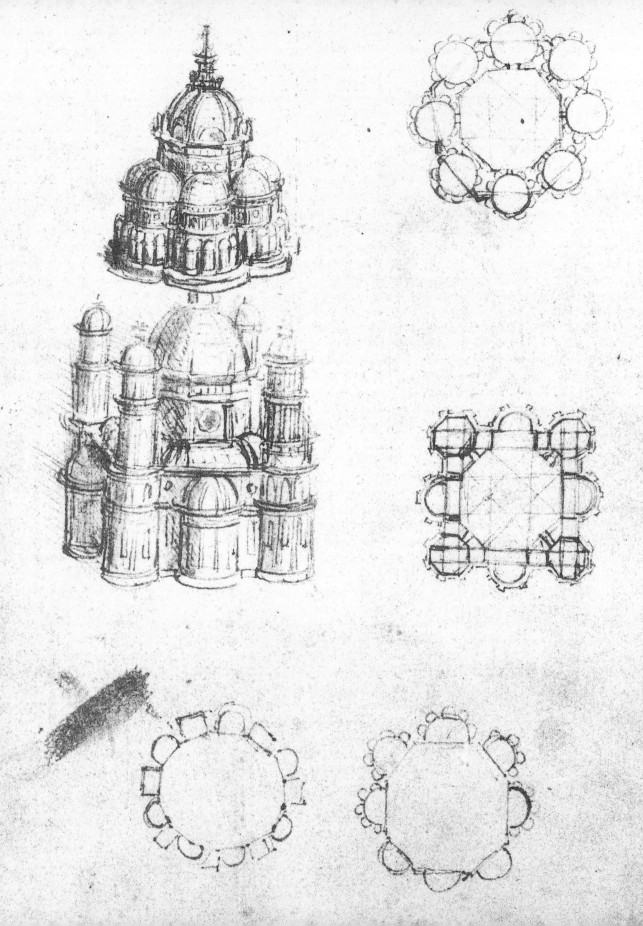

breeding grounds of disease. He writes of a 'congregation of people, herded together like goats, one behind the other, filling every corner with stench and spreading pestilence and death'.

So Leonardo set about designing a new kind of city, in which waste could be disposed of more easily, where miasma was less likely to form and where some of the population at least would be spared contact with decaying material. His city drawings are contained in the notebook known as Paris Manuscript B and now in the Institut de France in Paris. This fascinating manuscript contains a range of Leonardo drawings showing inventions such as flying machines and siege engines, as well as various architectural sketches.

Leonardo believed that upgrading the ventilation of buildings and improving the way people got rid of waste would help remove the miasma and make disease less likely to spread. Although the reasoning was based on bad science, the result was helpful because if you remove the waste you also get rid of a lot of germs. He thought he could build a city with some 30,000 dwellings that would be healthier than Milan and that would bring its lord not only fame but also what every ruler wants – a fortune in tax revenue.

The essence of Leonardo's ideal city design in his notebook was building the city on two different levels. At ground level are canals. As well as transporting goods, these would act as sewers, removing waste efficiently and keeping it away from a large proportion of the population, who would move around using spacious streets on the level above. There are also roads at the same level as the canals, for the use of wagons and carts delivering goods. 'Gentlemen' would use the upper streets, while servants and the 'lower orders' are restricted to the lower ones. Such a system would have been bad luck on the lower classes, carters and barge operators, but it was step in the right direction, and bargemen and river travellers were vulnerable anyway, because towns usually dumped sewage in rivers.

Up above, the streets are wide and the buildings reflect the elegant Renaissance style. Leonardo's drawing of a layered street shows a profusion of Classical arches and columns: 'Only let that which is good looking be seen on the surface of the city,' he writes. The width of the streets was a reaction against the narrow, crowded alleys of existing cities such as Milan. Wider streets would not only be comfortable, but would also give more space for air to circulate, allowing the miasma to escape and so reducing the risk of infection.

OPPOSITE *The cutaway drawing in Leonardo's notebook makes clear the city's two levels, with vaults and watercourse below and arcaded buildings above.*

To improve hygiene still more, Leonardo advocated regular street cleaning, and a full clean once a year, to remove miasma-harbouring rubbish. He designed a paddle-wheel system to pump water into the streets for cleaning. Each challenge, it seemed, drew further ideas from the master inventor. Since the waterways were also used for transport, there had to be a way of boats getting from the river to the city canals, which would be at a slightly higher level. Leonardo, therefore, designed a lock – strikingly similar to modern canal locks – to enable boats to travel in and out of the city's canal system.

Other refinements that Leonardo worked into his ideal city are houses with better ventilation, to remove or exclude miasma, and chimneys that sent smoke high up into the air, away from the city streets, thereby reducing pollution. There is also

A courtyard building (INSET), set well away from the main canal, is also built on multiple levels, as revealed in this modern model of Leonardo's design.

improved stabling for horses, with a stable block designed with the floor sloping towards a central channel, along which water could be sluiced, flushing away manure to the canals.

The split-level city survives only as a notebook sketch, although the artist did other architectural drawings, including some impressive ones of domed structures, to show the kinds of buildings he would have liked to construct. The city sketch is not fully realized and does not tell us exactly how the layout of the town was meant to work. The uses of the lower levels of buildings are not specified, for example – they may have been intended to service the upper-class houses above, but this is not clear. Leonardo probably never thought his city would actually be built. Like so many other drawings in his notebooks, from the helicopter to the submarines also found in Paris Manuscript B, the city sketch is a working drawing, showing the artist worrying away at ideas and responses to design or engineering challenges. As with so many of his drawings, though, the split-level city is far ahead of its time. As usual, Leonardo stops us in our tracks and makes us think about things in new and refreshing ways.

CHRISTIANOPOLIS

Johannes Valentinus Andreae, 1619

A Setting for Protestant Faith and Learning

Social reform and the advocacy of a particular set of beliefs
or way of life can sometimes have as strong an influence
on architecture as questions of style, structure or building
materials. And concerns of lifestyle and belief can sometimes
take planning outside the sphere of professional or qualified
architects, and into the hands of social reformers or
philosophers. A clear and little-known example of this is
Christianopolis, a concept for a town proposed by the German
writer and theologian Johannes Valentinus Andreae at the
beginning of the seventeenth century. It is a striking design –
ordered, symmetrical, with lots of green space and an unusual
emphasis on education and the equality of its citizens.

Andreae is known mainly as a Protestant theologian. He
was court preacher at Stuttgart and friend of the renowned
Humanist and scholar Erasmus of Rotterdam. Erasmus was
an important figure in the revival of scholarship who drove
the northern Renaissance in the Low Countries and Germany.
Andreae was a campaigner for better education, and was
unusual in his time in that he stressed the importance of science
as well as the humanities. Although he has been linked with
Renaissance secret societies such as the Rosicrucians, Andreae
seems to have been at heart a Protestant Christian, but one
with some interesting social ideas. One of these was the notion
of a utopian society of scholars or Christian brothers (a society
that has been compared to a Protestant monastery) who would
instigate a great reform of the church.

Andreae proposed housing his ideal society in a city
he called Christianopolis. The name is significant, in its
combination of the adjective Christian with the Greek polis
(city); the word thus links ancient Classical and modern
religious ideas, just as Renaissance philosophers such as
Erasmus would do. Andreae describes the city in a book,
published in 1619, called *Reipublicae Christianopolitanae
descriptio* (Description of the Republic of Christianopolis). The
book's title probably refers to the most ancient of all extended
accounts of an ideal state, Plato's Republic, and, like Plato's

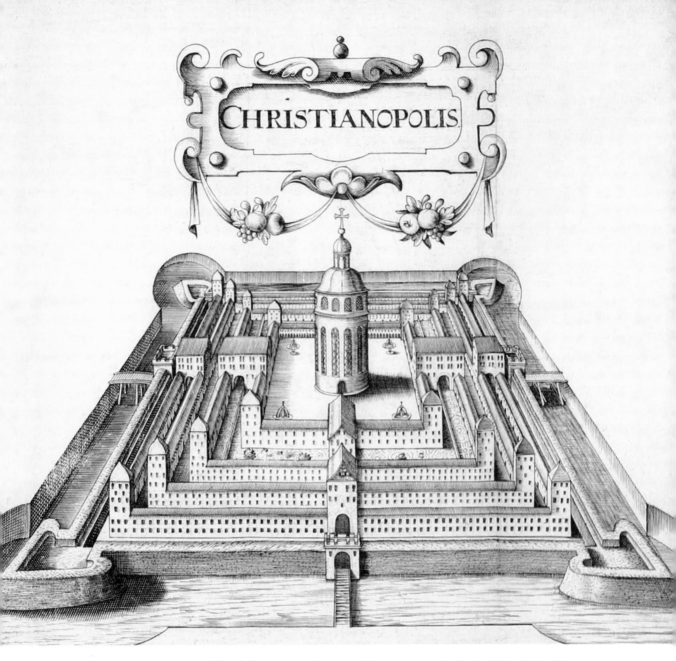

account, it concerns itself with the community as a whole, not just the architecture of the utopian city.

Unlike many utopians, Andreae visualizes a very specific architectural setting for his ideal city. It is to be built on a square plan, surrounded by a moat and a set of walls, with bastions at each corner – clearly this is a city that might need defending against attackers. Within the walls are four ranges of buildings planned as concentric squares – like college quadrangles but one within another – separated by gardens. At the very centre is a taller, circular building, looking out over

Andreae's 1619 book describing Christianopolis is illustrated with this aerial view of the city, which shows the layout very clearly but lacks fine architectural detail.

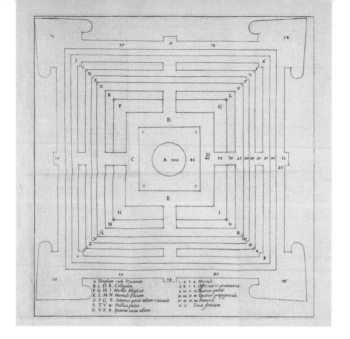

When he reproduced a plan of the city, Andreae provided a key so that the functions of the different structures were clear. The highly organized nature of the settlement was very important to its creator.

the whole complex like a watchtower. The outer quadrangle is used entirely for work and business, divided by function: farm buildings (barns, stables and granaries) to the east; mills, bakeries and other industries to the south; slaughterhouses, laundries, dairies and public kitchens to the north; and industries requiring heat or fire (forge, glassworks, brickworks and pottery) to the west.

The next quadrangles are residential. Nearly all the people were to live in small apartments or tenements, each consisting of a living room, bedroom and bathroom. These are minimalist dwellings without cooking facilities: people were expected to get their meals from the public kitchens. Compact dwellings were sufficient because the men and women in Andreae's ideal city would not accumulate possessions: '… these people draw together in what you might call a very suitable shell, where nothing is lacking which should cover a man and contain his belongings'. Conspicuous consumption was not to be encouraged. This would not be a place, Andreae says, where people 'heap up the baggage of iniquity'. Idleness would be discouraged, too. There are no leisured rich people in this somewhat socialist community: everyone would be a worker and contribute to the smooth running of the city.

The innermost quadrangle is known as the College. In tune with the scholarly and educational ideals of the northern Renaissance, this is in many ways the centre and hub of the whole city. On its upper floors is a school, which also has residential accommodation for the students. Beneath are public facilities – a library, a laboratory and a printing press. All these rooms look out on the round tower at the centre of the complex. Andreae sometimes calls this the citadel – although it did not have the military function that this name implies, being a combination of church and city hall.

Between these buildings the space is mostly green. Andreae valued gardens not just because they were productive and attractive, but also for their educational importance. So the gardens include communal spaces containing botanical specimens (for scientific interest but arranged so that they look beautiful), medicinal plants, aviaries and beehives, in addition to other gardens, which are allocated in sections to the residents so that everyone has a small patch of land. People were expected to get around the city on foot, and many of the quadrangles have arcades, like Italian Renaissance city buildings, to shelter pedestrians.

If this suggests a place where the environment was considered important, other things point to that, too. Andreae stresses the benefits of good ventilation and proposes to pipe water directly into the apartments (this at a time when most people, even in towns, had to fetch their water from a well or pump). Fireproofing was considered vital, with masonry walls separating apartments. There is even a proposed central heating system powered by a public furnace, though Andreae does not provide details of how it would work.

The architecture is mostly, as far as one can see from Andreae's illustration, plain and simple. The long ranges of buildings are punctuated by towers, useful to keep a lookout on the surrounding areas. The fronts and backs of the houses look the same – Andreae's Protestant sensibility shunned the idea of putting up an impressive front because it was education and spiritual wellbeing that counted, not fancy facades. The arcades and the great curving mass of the central building add visual interest.

In Christianopolis, Andreae took the ancient concept of the ideal city – inherited from philosophers such as Plato and filtered through the ideas of Italian Renaissance artists such as Martini (see Ideal City entry on page 26) – and gave it a northern, Protestant ethos. He proposed a plain but highly ordered architecture to house an unpretentious and ordered society. Here, because there were no idle rich, people's working hours would be shorter. It sounds a little like twentieth-century socialism – with similarly plain-vanilla architecture – but with a revolutionary emphasis on education. This, at least, was a lesson that was worth preserving.

CHAPTER 2
ENLIGHTENED VISIONS,

The seventeenth and eighteenth intellectual change.

Scientists such as Galileo and Isaac Newton were transforming the way we look at the cosmos. Philosophers and writers, especially members of the movement known as the Enlightenment in France, were questioning the accepted truths of religion. Architects were extending and rebuilding the world's great cities, from St Petersburg to Washington DC.

Many of the new city developments were in the classical style, which the architects used for everything from small houses to vast cathedrals. Building in the Classical style was in part about adapting the proportions and details of ancient buildings to make structures fit for modern life – churches with Corinthian columns, or houses with rooms shaped as perfect cubes or double cubes. But the architects of the Enlightenment period often pushed the style in new directions, sometimes taking it to levels that were too daring to be practical. Inigo Jones's plans for the royal Whitehall Palace in London, for example, were too vast for even the lavish spending levels of the Stuart monarchy. Sir Christopher Wren's 'Great Model' design for St Paul's Cathedral, London was not orthodox enough for the conservative clergy of the time.

ECCENTRIC SPACES

centuries were times of seismic

Designs such as Jones's and Wren's, though, look traditional beside some of the proposed buildings of the eighteenth century. In France, especially, designers such as Étienne-Louis Boullée produced truly bizarre buildings such as his Cenotaph for Isaac Newton, a spherical, windowless building intended to project an image of the cosmos on its vast curving interior walls. Designs such as this and Charles Ribart's extraordinary building in the shape of an elephant, proposed for central Paris, were visionary creations that were simply too unusual to get farther than the drawing board. But even the elephant, probably the least likely building in this book and the one that looks most like a joke, inspired a later builder in North America to produce a structure in the same form.

However, the lasting influence of architects such as Boullée and Ledoux is not in direct imitations – buildings like the Newton monument are too much products of their times for that. The reason they still compel attention is in part their immaculate draughtsmanship, in part their purity of form and in part that they encourage architects and designers to think differently, to question orthodoxy and to try original forms. This is what takes people back again and again to the often beautifully drawn plans of the Enlightenment period.

WHITEHALL PALACE

Inigo Jones, 1622–38

A Grand Palace for an Absolute Monarch

The Scottish king James VI, who became James I of England, had the grandest architectural plans of any British monarch, but the building that was to be his most magnificent home did not start out as a royal palace at all. Its story began in the thirteenth century, when the Archbishop of York acquired a plot of land in Westminster, on the site of the present Whitehall, and built himself a town house called York Place. York Place continued as the residence of high-ranking churchmen, and by the time of Henry VIII it had passed into the hands of the most

The design for the vast palace at Whitehall was one of Inigo Jones's most famous and was often reproduced after his death. This engraving was produced for King George II and later published in a book by the British architect William Kent in 1770.

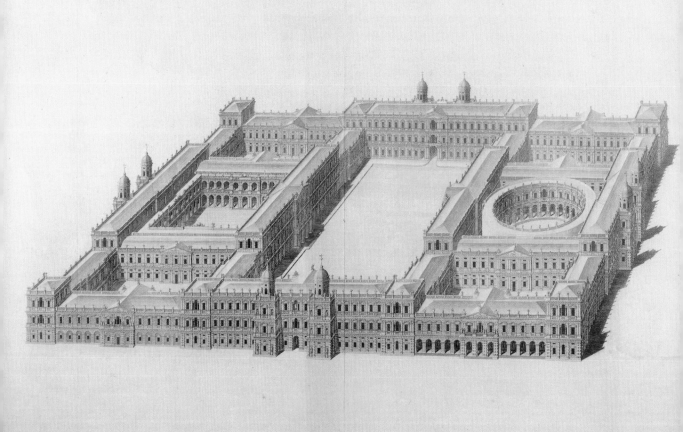

Of His Britannick Majesty's Palace of White Hall, Charing Cross Side.

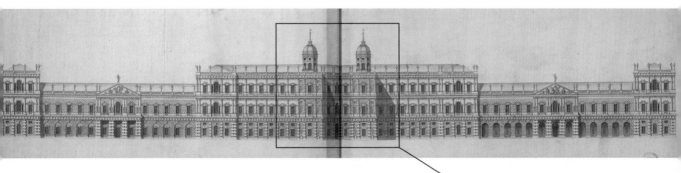

powerful prelate of the period, Cardinal Wolsey, who hugely extended it, turning it into one of the largest houses in London. In the late 1520s, Wolsey and Henry clashed and Wolsey fell from power. Henry seized his properties, so both his vast house at Hampton Court and York Place became royal palaces. It was in Henry's time that York Place became known as Whitehall, on account of the pale stone of which it was built.

Henry enlarged and extended Whitehall still further, adding a host of facilities to accommodate his various enthusiasms, such as a tiltyard for jousting, a court for his favourite game – 'real' tennis – and a bowling green. The few contemporary images of the complex show an agglomeration of courtyards, gables, towers, turrets, chimneys and gatehouses – it was a typical Tudor great house, probably looking rather like the older parts of Hampton Court.

This irregular hotchpotch did not suit the first Stuart monarch. In 1614, James hired Inigo Jones as Surveyor to the King's Works, and, a few years later, Jones was given the task of rebuilding Whitehall to make a residence fit for a seventeenth-century king with very grand ideas. Jones was the ideal man for this job, being a follower of the latest Italian architectural fashion. As a young man he had visited Italy twice. He studied drawing there, and examined many new buildings in the Classical style as well as looking at ancient ruins. In Venice he met Vincenzo Scamozzi, the pupil and colleague of the great Italian architect Andrea Palladio, seizing the opportunity to buy many of Palladio's drawings, which were in Scamozzi's possession. In addition, Jones studied the works of the Roman writer on architecture, Vitruvius, and the books of modern Italian architects and architectural writers such as Sebastiano Serlio. Jones was thus the one British person with a clear, informed knowledge of the Classical architecture of Palladio – a style featuring strict symmetry, flat roofs and Classical columns.

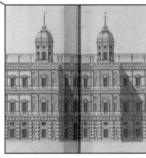

A detail from a principal facade shows one of the pairs of towers (INSET) topped with cupolas that flank the entrances to the palace.

The only part of the new palace of Whitehall to be built – the Banqueting House – showed off this new style to perfection. A plain street front with regular rows of windows beneath an apparently flat roof and displaying only very restrained decoration conceals a much more elaborate and richly decorative interior. This opulent room was intended both for banquets and for performances of court masques, which were elaborate theatrical entertainments that presented thinly disguised royal propaganda, for which Jones designed the sets and costumes. But the Banqueting House was intended to be only a small part of a vast rebuilt Whitehall Palace, in the Classical Palladian style. The new palace that Jones conceived occupied a site between the River Thames and today's St James's Park, with the modern street of Whitehall running somewhere through the middle.

The proposed building is an enormous structure, arranged around seven main courtyards – six rectangular and one circular – all in the Classical style. It has vast facades to the river and the park sides, and slightly shorter ones to the other two sides. The Banqueting House was to be one tiny part of this structure – its grand facade is just seven windows wide, whereas the plans for the palace show fronts with forty or fifty windows on each main floor.

The Scottish writer Charles Mackay, in his 1840 book *The Thames and its Tributaries*, provides a brief description of the layout of the vast building: 'The palace was to have consisted of four fronts, each with an entrance between two towers. Within these were to have been one large central court and five smaller ones, and between two of the latter a handsome circus [circular courtyard], with an arcade below, supported by pillars in the form of caryatides. The whole length of the palace was

The Banqueting House, the one part of the palace to be built, is dominated by the ceiling painting, The Apotheosis of James I, *by Rubens.*

to have been 1,152ft [351m], and its depth 872ft [266m].' The overall impression was one of grandeur, symmetry, order and repetition – long rows of windows relieved by the occasional tower. It was the total antithesis of the old Whitehall, with its apparently random collection of structures.

It is hard to exaggerate how shockingly new and different this building would have looked in the middle of seventeenth-century London. Most of the city consisted of narrow streets of timber-framed buildings, with a little brick and stone here and there; the architecture was a mixture of English traditional styles, with a generous sprinkling of Gothic medieval churches. People had been building in this way for centuries, but Whitehall Palace signalled the arrival of a new, Palladian style that was totally different, even alien, in its order and hard-edged symmetry.

After the accession of James's son, Charles I, came the English Civil War. All royal building came to a halt and the Banqueting House remained the only part of the scheme to be built. The vast Stuart palace was almost forgotten. The old hotchpotch remained, with alterations by Sir Christopher Wren in the 1680s, when James II and VII was on the throne. However, his successors, William and Mary, preferred the smaller Kensington Palace to Whitehall, so the old building fell out of favour. In 1691, it was damaged in a fire and further fire in 1698 destroyed most of the remaining palace except for the Banqueting House and one or two other buildings.

Since the late seventeenth century, the British monarchy followed William and Mary's lead and shunned vast palaces. Many of the rulers of the past three centuries have preferred life on a domestic scale, and, although Windsor Castle is large, it is another architectural hotchpotch, like Whitehall Palace once was. The country's two longest-lived rulers, Victoria and Elizabeth II, have both expressed a preference for smaller houses such as Balmoral, Sandringham or Victoria and Albert's Italianate 'villa' Osborne on the Isle of Wight. As a result, Britain has no royal palace on the scale of France's Versailles or Spain's Escorial. Some historians have believed that this penchant for a low-key royal family, with plenty of pomp and ceremony but without the lavish architectural indulgence of kings such as France's Louis XIV, has helped Britain keep its monarchy and avoid revolutions. It may be that the loss of the architectural grandeur that James I craved has been to the benefit of his successors.

ST PAUL'S CATHEDRAL

Christopher Wren, 1670–4

The Bold and Original Cathedral that Sir Christopher Wren Really Wanted to Build

In every crisis there is an opportunity. In 1666, London faced the biggest crisis of its history: the great fire that destroyed much of the city from the Tower of London in the east to the Temple area in the west. Houses, shops, inns – mostly timber-framed buildings and many with thatched roofs – were laid low. Dozens of churches, even though they had stone walls, were beyond repair. And the great medieval Cathedral of St Paul was very badly damaged.

In this disaster the architect Christopher Wren saw the biggest opportunity of his career. Hardly was the fire out before he was designing a plan for a rebuilt city, a beautiful Classical layout with new streets and squares. The plan was rejected: property owners objected to the necessary relocations and rejigging – they wanted to waste no time getting back into business, at their accustomed addresses, where customers could be sure to find them. However, Wren won the commission to design fifty new churches. Meanwhile, the cathedral was patched up so that services could resume.

Old St Paul's had been built between the eleventh and thirteenth centuries, and was extended in the later Middle Ages. Like most English cathedrals, it was a long, cross-shaped building. It had a tall, central spire, which dominated the London skyline. By the early 1600s, the building had fallen into disrepair, so the architect Inigo Jones had restored it, adding an entrance portico with Classical columns at the west end. The old cathedral was, therefore, in a mixture of architectural styles, but in essence it was a medieval cathedral, with rows of arches, large stained-glass windows and a longitudinal plan. It was very traditional.

By the end of the 1660s, it was becoming clear to the cathedral authorities that the old, patched-up cathedral would need rebuilding. They wrote to Wren requesting a new design, and he set to work, proposing a cathedral in the Classical style, with Roman columns, semicircular arches and a dome instead of a spire. This first design was quite small and it was rejected

as too modest. As Wren puts it, some people thought the design 'was not stately enough, and contended, that for the Honour of the Nation, and City of London, it ought not to be exceeded in magnificence, by any Church in Europe'. In addition, the cathedral authorities had scope to be more ambitious, because in 1670 a new Rebuilding Act allocated more money for the new cathedral.

So Wren began again, this time proposing a design planned like a Greek cross, with short arms and a large, central dome. The heart of the building is a vast space under the central dome. At the west end is a vestibule, itself roofed by a smaller dome. The whole effect of this centralized plan was quite unlike the elongated churches that were traditional in England. But as Wren developed the design in detail, it seemed to work. The king, Archbishop Sheldon and Dean Sancroft approved, and the job of demolishing Old St Paul's progressed

Elements such as columns, carved capitals and the ornate lanterns at the top of each dome are represented in painstaking detail in the Great Model.

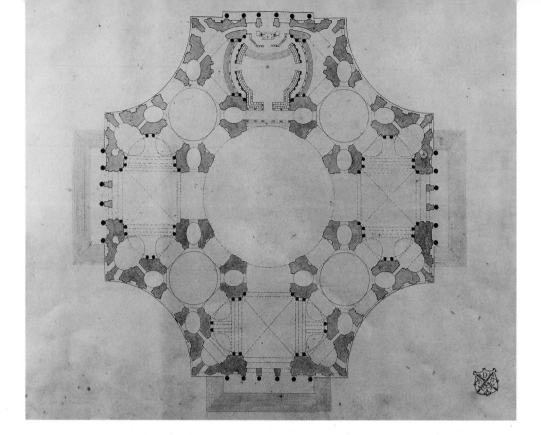

Wren's plan shows how he envisaged a symmetrical layout with a vast space for the congregation at the very centre of the cathedral, beneath the main dome.

– with the aid of dynamite and, when the explosions and flying masonry alarmed the people living nearby, a battering ram.

At last, in 1673, Wren was officially appointed architect, charged with directing the construction of the new building and answerable to a Royal Commission, whose members included numerous bishops and archbishops together with the Lord Chancellor, the Lord Treasurer and representatives of the City of London. As a further seal of approval, at the end of the year, Wren was knighted.

A key clause in Wren's agreement with the Commission was that he should produce a model of the new cathedral to act as a reference for the architect and builders. The model is made in wood and to a large scale, some 20½ft (6.3m) long and 12ft (3.6m) high – not for nothing has it been known ever since as the Great Model. This enormous wooden construction is a triumph in itself – it is beautifully made by a team led by joiner William Cleere. The exterior is immaculately finished, showing to advantage the high, concave-curving walls with their Classical details and the enormous dome rising above them. The vestibule at the west end of the building is the main entrance. It is fronted by a portico with a row of gigantic Corinthian columns – as grand an entrance to a major building as could be. There are also entrances in the north and south facades – these provide a focus for the sides of the building as well as improving circulation.

The interior of the model is no less impressive, giving a sense of the truly cavernous space within the building. The choir is in the eastern arm of the building, with the congregation assembling in the huge space beneath the dome and spreading out into the north and south arms of the structure. The interior details are painstakingly represented in the model – craftsmen were paid for carving some 350 capitals, a plasterer was employed and gilders made the architecture still richer.

Wren must have been very pleased but the Commissioners were not. When they saw the model they had cold feet, particularly the clergy, who felt that the design was too foreign, too popish and just not traditional enough. They were also concerned that the structure would take too long to build – they wanted to resume services as soon as possible. With a conventional building, it was possible to build and roof the choir and start using it while construction of the nave went on beyond a temporary partition. When almost the whole building was beneath a vast dome, it couldn't be used until the dome was finished. The Commissioners demanded a rethink.

So the Great Model design, which Wren thought his best work and which had been hailed as a future glory for the capital, was never built at full size. It remains a reality only in Wren's drawings and Cleere's magnificent version in wood. Devastated, Wren went away and produced an alternative design, known now as the Warrant Design, which the Commissioners accepted. Compared to the Great Model, a design of great purity, the Warrant Design is a bizarre collection of disparate parts, an elongated building with a dome that turns into a spire halfway up. But for all its oddity, the Commissioners approved and Wren went ahead.

However, St Paul's did not end up like the Warrant Design. When the plan was accepted, Wren secured an agreement that he could alter the design as he went along. He took full advantage of this, changing the design of the dome radically and modifying the west end to create the entrance front that is so familiar today. The finished St Paul's is still a compromise between a centralized domed building and the elongated plan preferred by the clergy, but it is a compromise that works and that has become the most famous church in Britain and a symbol for London. The Great Model remains in the cathedral as a reminder of the purer, more radical design that might have been.

THE TRIUMPHAL ELEPHANT

Charles-François Ribart de Chamoust, 1758

A Monument to Honour Louis XV

Buildings in the shape of animals have been around for a long time. Like the Big Duck built on Long Island, New York, in 1931, they are usually elaborate jokes, designed to catch the eyes of passers-by. So when in 1758 a French architect proposed constructing a building in the shape of an elephant right in the middle of Paris, on the Champs Élysées, where the Arc de Triomphe now stands, it looked like the biggest joke of all. However, its designer, Charles-François Ribart de Chamoust, was deadly serious. He intended it as a sincere tribute to the French king himself.

People have always been fascinated by elephants – their size, their power and strength, the contrasting flexibility and sensitivity of their trunks, their usefulness as beasts of burden and war. Although elephants were rarely seen in Europe, a few found their way into royal and imperial collections and zoos. Artists admired them and sometimes used them as exotic symbols of strength – Bernini produced an elephant sculpture in 1667, on which he mounted an ancient Egyptian obelisk to form a monument that still stands in the Piazza della Minerva in Rome. No wonder that this massive and noble beast became a symbol of royalty and of the power of the king.

It was thinking like this that inspired Ribart to suggest his monument in the form of an elephant. Spurning conventional ideas such as triumphal arches or equestrian statues, Ribart proposed a multi-storeyed, elephant-shaped building, with rooms inside accessed from a central staircase, and an eye-catching fountain emerging from the trunk. He dubbed it 'Grand kiosque, à la gloire du roi' (Great booth dedicated to the glory of the king).

What kind of person could come up with an idea like this? Ribart is a shadowy figure. Even his first names are not known for certain and he is recognized more for his architectural writings than for his buildings. He was fascinated by architecture's ancient origins and was one of those who thought that the column, one of the most basic elements of architecture, derived from the tree. Many people have seen similarities

Ribart published several images of The Triumphal Elephant, including this cross-section revealing the arrangement of rooms on either side of the central staircase.

between cathedrals, with their rows of columns, and forests, but Ribart took this farther. In a book called *L'Ordre François Trouvé dans la Nature* (1776), he suggests that the three main parts of a column – the base, shaft and capital – derive from the three

Ribart's book L'Ordre François Trouvé dans la Nature, *his description of his French order of architecture, shows how he traced the origins of the column and capital to the roots, trunk and foliage of a tree.*

parts of a tree: the roots visible just above the ground; the trunk; and the crown of foliage. He even designed a 'French Order' of column based on this theory, arranging the columns in clusters of three, to suggest the way trees often grow in small groups.

It could not have been a huge leap for someone who thought about the parallels between nature and architecture in this way to hit upon the idea of designing an entire building in the shape of an animal. The large and powerful elephant must have seemed a fitting choice for a royal monument.

The elephant was triumphal in the sense that it represented the triumphs of war: it was to be shown as if returning from a victory, bearing a figure of the king himself surrounded with the spoils of war. It is the height of a five-storey building and would have made a startling focal point for the Champs Élysées. In the mid-eighteenth century, this was a less urban setting than it is now. It had been laid out by André Le Nôtre, gardener to Louis XIV, in 1667 and was lined with kitchen gardens and groves. The great intersection of the Étoile was not paved until 1777, and the Champs Élysées itself was not built up until the Napoleonic period at the beginning of the nineteenth century. Ribart's elephant would have stood out against greenery and formal groves of trees, an admirable setting for the noble beast, mounted with the figure of the king, that would be visible from some way off.

Extraordinary from the outside, the elephant is no less astounding within. The creature's body houses two floors, with the main rooms on the upper floor, occupying both the body and the head. The dining room is decorated to resemble part of a great forest, with trees (irregularly planted) instead of columns around the walls, and punctuated with stones, including a buffet in the form of a large rock. A stream runs around the room, freshening the atmosphere inside according to Ribart. Indirect lighting (with daylight entering the room only via reflections) enhances the forest atmosphere. Chairs, tables and other furniture could be folded away into the walls and floors.

The other main room on the upper floor is the ballroom or throne room. It is adorned with grotesque figures and a pair of murals representing the Past and the Future. Ribart also suggested that there should be lights that imitated the movements of the stars or planets. Adjacent is a smaller room or cabinet, which could be used as a buffet when balls were in progress.

The ballroom is large enough to contain a sizeable assembly and an orchestra. In a curious inversion of function, Ribart proposed to install megaphone-like devices in the elephant's ears, so that they would broadcast the orchestra's music to the outside world. The effect, both visual and sonic, of this bizarre building would have been unlike anything else.

The Triumphal Elephant was only ever a proposal. Paris eventually made do with the imposing but conventional Arc de Triomphe that stands in its place. But the idea of elephantine architecture was not quite dead. Napoleon had plans to revive the idea and commissioned the Éléphant de la Bastille on the site of the former prison, stormed during the revolution. This was never built in its planned form, although a full-scale plaster model was constructed, and stood on the Bastille site until 1846.

A more modest but also bizarre elephant-building, now known as 'Lucy the Elephant', was built to advertise real estate in Margate City, New Jersey in 1881. This structure of wooden and metal sheeting has rooms inside its body and a viewing platform in the howdah, where its builder, James V. Lafferty, took clients to look at nearby parcels of land. No longer used for this purpose, Lucy remains as a reminder of one American's whim and an echo of a still more visionary project conceived more than a century earlier.

Napoleon's proposed monument at the Bastille was similar in form and size to Ribart's design, and used his idea of the fountain coming from the trunk, but was not intended to have rooms inside.

ARC-ET-SENANS, FRANCE
ROYAL SALTWORKS
Claude Nicolas Ledoux, 1770s

*An Ideal City Combining Symbolism and
Rationalism in its Design*

The French architect Claude Nicolas Ledoux was one of the
noted Neo-Classicists of the eighteenth century, who designed
châteaux, town houses and a series of tax offices built around
the edge of Paris, to facilitate the collection of customs duties
on goods entering the city. He was seen as an establishment
figure, employed by the French monarchy, but he was also an
enthusiast for a way of architectural thinking that was very
different from the mainstream – the notion of *architecture*

parlante (architecture that speaks the story of its function through its appearance). One of the great unrealized works of *architecture parlante* was Ledoux's plan for the Royal Saltworks and associated buildings at Arc-et-Senans, which took an extraordinary form, unlike any other town before or since.

Ledoux was appointed inspector to the Royal Saltworks of Lorraine and the Franche-Comté, eastern France, in 1771. When he visited the saltworks at Salins-les-Bains, he was shocked by the dark, choking atmosphere that he found: the place reminded him of hell. Two years after his appointment, he was in a position to do something about this, because he was admitted to the Royal Academy of Architecture, which placed him among the elite of French architects. This gave him the status to produce plans for royal buildings, and he set about planning a new saltworks that would be lighter, better ventilated and more efficient. An early decision was to move the works northwest to Arc-et-Senans, closer to the Forest of Chaux, the source of fuel for the works. Ledoux argued that it was easier to divert the flow of water than to transport heavy loads of wood 12 miles (20km) or more. He also found a good, flat site near the forest.

The buildings that Ledoux constructed there show his dramatic handling of the Classical style. The columns of the dominant building – the Director's House – are astonishing. From a distance they seem horizontally striped; closer to, they are revealed to be made up of alternate round and square blocks, which at once break up their outline and make them look more massive. They certainly convey a sense of awe and grandeur that is quite fitting for the person in charge of an important royal enterprise.

But Ledoux's sense in which the architecture speaks its meaning goes beyond this kind of symbolism. *Architecture parlante* can take many forms. It can be simply ornamental such as American architect Benjamin Latrobe's invention of 'American orders', in which the acanthus foliage on Classical capitals is replaced by something obviously local, such as corn cobs. It can, though, go much farther and involve the very form a building takes, and this was the idea that engaged Ledoux. So the imposing Director's House is approached through an entrance archway that is built like a cave, with bizarre, rubble-like masonry above the gate. The effect is one of leaving behind a primitive world and entering Ledoux's world of regulated, sophisticated Classicism.

OPPOSITE *The saltworks and its related buildings were planned to form a great circle. At the very centre is the Director's House (*INSET*), one of the buildings that was completed, with its massive columned portico.*

France's rulers were absolute monarchs, who used cosmic symbolism, so it was fitting that the Royal Saltworks should have a cosmic plan. Ledoux said that the shape of the complex should be 'as pure as the one of the sun during its journey' and he laid the site out with a plan resembling a sundial. The buildings are carefully placed within this solar layout. When the sun is at its height, in the middle of the day, it is right above the Director's House. At the end of the day it reaches the clerk's office in the western part of the site, because the clerk is the last person to be at work, writing up the records of the day's production.

The architect was not completely bound up with symbolism. Many aspects of the design are functional. Accommodation buildings and offices are carefully distanced from the noxious fumes produced by salt production, and there is an attempt to place buildings appropriately for their purpose. However, if it is rational, the layout also has its faults: the workers found themselves with cramped accommodation.

*The Oikema or 'House of pleasure' is at first glance a rectangular courtyard building (*BELOW LEFT *and* BOTTOM*). However, on closer examination, the phallic shape of the central section (*BELOW RIGHT*) is very clear.*

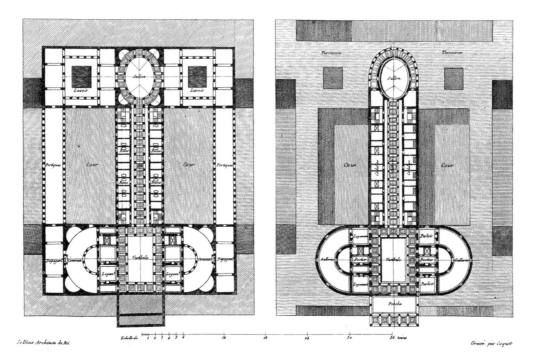

Ledoux's ordered solar system of a plan was conceived in the 1770s. But in 1791 revolution overturned France and brought a republic in its wake. Ledoux did not abandon his plans for the saltworks, however, but extended them with a series of structures that amounted to an ideal town, full of the most amazing and bizarre examples of *architecture parlante*. This remained on Ledoux's drawing board but it was full of remarkable might-have-beens. One of these is the house of the River Superintendent, which is built directly over the river. The water flows through the middle of the structure, emerging as a rushing waterfall, both drawing attention to the building and its purpose, and providing the occupant with a perfect observation point, so that the building works both symbolically and functionally. Its shape – the whole building takes the form of a great arch – also reflects Ledoux's love of strong geometrical forms.

Sometimes, a structure's plan reflects its purpose. A unique example is the building Ledoux referred to as the Oikema, a 'house of pleasure' or 'temple of sexual instruction', the plan of which takes the form of an erect penis. Scholars sometimes interpret this as some kind of temple, though the most down-to-earth interpretation of this building with many small rooms is the most likely – it was almost certainly intended to be a brothel.

The planned structures at Arc-et-Senans also included two that took spherical form. One is a small house allocated to a farm manager. The other, much grander and more astonishing, is the cemetery. To build a house of the dead in the form of a sphere was a symbolic statement. The sphere was seen as the most perfect of geometrical forms, and was also a medieval image of the cosmos. It would have sat well in the town of Arc-et-Senans, with its solar plan, although it could have been eclipsed by a still more striking spherical building – Étienne-Louis Boullée's Cenotaph for Isaac Newton (see Cenotaph for Isaac Newton entry on page 60).

Designs such as these, together with the structures that were completed, ensure that the saltworks are still a source of fascination. As one of the first attempts to design a factory rationally, and as one of the most densely symbolic of all architectural projects, Arc-et-Senans keeps it place in the sun.

CENOTAPH FOR ISAAC NEWTON

Étienne-Louis Boullée, 1784

A Spherical Monument Taller than the Great Pyramid

In 1784, a set of architectural drawings by a little-known French architect appeared that were shocking in form and scale. Among the drawings, by Étienne-Louis Boullée, were some featuring a building shaped as a huge perfect sphere. The drawing was described as a cenotaph, or empty tomb, for Isaac Newton. This impossible-looking structure was never built, but it has haunted architects ever since. To discover why, we have to see Boullée's sphere in the context of its time.

Eighteenth-century Europe was dominated by the movement in philosophy and science called the Enlightenment. The philosophers of the Enlightenment questioned the old moral authorities – especially the church – and insisted that rationalism was the best basis for human thought and conduct. A major centre of the Enlightenment movement was France, home to philosophers and writers such as Voltaire and Diderot. And there was more than rationalism in the air. People began to strive for a new social order, too, in which human rights would be upheld and power would be taken away from the aristocracy and the church.

How might architecture respond to this change? One of the people to address this question was Boullée, who rejected as frivolous the prevailing highly ornate Rococo style, associated with the pleasure palaces of kings and aristocrats, and advocated a return to the Classical orders of ancient Greece and Rome. He was also keen on the idea of taking architectural forms from nature and from 'pure' geometry. Boullée was an academic who did not complete many major buildings. But the projects that he published are extraordinary, and the most remarkable of all is the cenotaph for the British mathematician, astronomer and physicist Sir Isaac Newton, who had died in 1727.

Newton was one of the most influential of all scientists, and a leading intellectual of his time. His work spanned mechanics, optics and calculus, and his laws of motion and universal gravitation are fundamental to the way we

OVERLEAF *Boullée's most famous drawing of the monument is dramatically lit to bring out the curving surface of the sphere. Small groups of figures on the lower and middle levels emphasize the structure's vast scale.*

VUE INTÉRIEURE DU CÉNOTAPHE DE NEWTON

understand the physical world. This work, and Newton's
method of underpinning his discoveries about the world
with mathematical proof, made him a key figure in the
Enlightenment.

   To commemorate this stellar figure, Boullée conceived
a truly cosmic building, a monument in the form of a huge
empty mausoleum. It took the shape of an enormous stone

*During the day the sun shone
through small holes in the
surface of the sphere, giving
the impression of the sky at
night, arching high above the
platform containing the scientist's
empty tomb.*

sphere, hollow inside, girdled by circular platforms and rows of cypress trees. It was a sphere for reasons of symbolism and sheer visual effect. Boullée writes: 'The shape of the sphere offers the greatest surface to the eye, and this lends it majesty. It has the utmost simplicity, because that surface is flawless and endless.' The combination of majesty and apparent endlessness made for a remarkable design.

Looking at Boullée's drawings, it is difficult at first for the viewer to get their bearings until it dawns on them that the tiny specks about one-third of the way up are human figures approaching a doorway. These figures give an idea of the scale of the great sphere: it was planned to be some 500ft (150m) in diameter. In the 1780s, the world's tallest buildings were Strasbourg Cathedral, at 466ft (142m) and the Great Pyramid at Giza, at 455ft (139m). Boullée's cenotaph would, therefore, have been the world's tallest building, vaster by far than any tomb of king or emperor, greater than any cathedral or shrine.

From the outside, the building is obviously a sphere, although the lower half is concealed by the surrounding platforms and plinths, so that it appears to emerge from them. The bottom part of the volume is implied by a pair of curving ramps, and it is easy to get the idea that this building is at heart one great pure form. There is no ornament, no Rococo carving, not even the more restrained ornament of the Classical style, to distract the visitor's attention from the simplicity and purity.

The platforms and plinths are planted with cypress trees (a traditional symbol of mourning) and the middle platform (one-third of the way up) leads to an entrance. However, Boullée seems to have intended the main way into the cenotaph to be at the base of the building, where a semicircular portal forms the prelude to a long corridor leading to the interior.

Inside, the visitor to Newton's shrine would have the unearthly experience of standing inside a cavernous spherical space. The entrance corridor leads to a platform at the bottom of the sphere, where the sarcophagus is placed. Above, the spherical walls curve upwards. They are pierced with tiny holes, which let in daylight and are placed so that what opened up above one's head was the image of a starry night, with the Moon, planets and constellations glittering in the darkness. The visitor stood at the heart of the universe that Newton's work explained so rationally. At night the interior works differently. An illuminated armillary sphere hanging at the very centre of the building sends an eerie glow towards the walls.

Boullée's drawings of the monument – exterior views, plans and sections – were circulated widely in the years after he produced them in 1784. The architect's work as a teacher (at the École Nationale des Ponts et Chaussés), the connections he had made as architect to Frederick II of Prussia and his fame in France meant that he had a large network of contacts. Contemporaries were impressed, but did not immediately start to design buildings in the form of gigantic spheres or other plain geometrical forms. However, Boullée was part of a movement that made architects turn more to plainer, Classical design and away from the frills and furbelows of Rococo.

Boullée has also had a more recent influence. His works were published widely in the twentieth century, and have inspired architects such as the Italian postmodernist Aldo Rossi, many of whose buildings (and designs for household objects such as tableware and coffee pots) marry purity of form with lack of ornament in a distinctly Boullée-like way. The Cenotaph for Isaac Newton, disturbing in its form and eerie in its interior, is a shining example of the way phantom architecture from long ago can continue to provoke and stimulate the mind.

NATIONAL LIBRARY

Étienne-Louis Boullée, 1785

The Ultimate Enlightenment Library

A national library is more than a place to store a large collection of books. It is also a home of learning, a gathering place for scholars and an important national symbol. One of the first countries to have such as library was France, where the architect Étienne-Louis Boullée created one of his greatest designs to house it. Around 330ft (100m) long, with a huge arching vault and bookcases arranged in tiers, it would have been the biggest and most imposing reading room in the world.

The library began as the royal collection of books and manuscripts in the Middle Ages. The collection grew steadily, and the growth was accelerated in the seventeenth century under Louis XIII and Louis XIV, especially during the time of Jean-Baptiste Colbert, who served for a long period as Louis XIV's Finance Minister and was a keen collector of books. As it expanded, the collection moved several times to various locations in Paris, and by the late seventeenth century was housed in the rue Vivienne. In 1692, the library took the momentous step of opening its doors to the public.

By this time, there had already been plans to move the books to still larger, purpose-built premises, but nothing came of these schemes, and as expansion continued into the eighteenth century the library became overcrowded and the need for a larger building was still more pressing. Various sites and ideas were proposed, and the architect who worked hardest to come up with a new design was Étienne-Louis Boullée.

Several challenges faced a designer of the new library: finding a suitable site, accommodating a huge number of books, providing space for readers, keeping the budget down and producing a building impressive enough to house one of the world's greatest bibliographic collections. Boullée's design addressed these challenges ingeniously. The architect found his site not by acquiring new land or demolishing existing buildings, but by proposing to roof over a long courtyard, about 330ft (100m) long and 100ft (30m) across, to create one enormous room. He designed an arching vault to go over the courtyard, its coffered ceiling creating the appropriate sense

of grandeur, and pierced this with a large skylight. Rows of bookshelves arranged in tiers lines the long sides of the room, leaving a generous circulation space in the middle.

Boullée's plan answered the challenges well. He could house a vast number of books (perhaps up to 300,000 volumes) and managed to fill the space with natural light from above, overcoming the problem that there could be no side windows in a room surrounded by existing buildings and lined with bookshelves. His design was visually very impressive. And because it reused the existing courtyard, it was much cheaper than a new, free-standing building would have been – one contemporary estimated Boullée's proposal would cost only one-tenth the price of a completely new building.

The books are on open-access shelves, facing the visitor. This was in marked contrast to the old medieval way of housing books, with each volume attached to the bookcase by a chain. Although ancient, the chained library system was still

Boullée depicted the interior of the library as a vast empty space, in which scholars could meet and talk. The poses of some of the figures resemble the philosophers of ancient Greece portrayed in Raphael's painting The School of Athens.

widely used, and the method of storage in Boullée's library was a way of making the collection more accessible than in many libraries. To emphasize this point, Boullée's drawings show visitors wandering freely about the space. However, he illustrates no desks where readers could work – a strange omission, although the wide floor space could have been used to accommodate desks and chairs.

The architectural style of the interior is Classical – a sober version of the style with very plain Tuscan or Doric columns and Atlas statues. The great arching ceiling, creating a volume in the form of a half cylinder, reflects Boullée's interest in pure geometry, as in his Newton monument (see Cenotaph for Isaac Newton entry on page 60). The top lighting was both practical and a testimony to another of Boullée's great interests, what he called 'the architecture of shadows', or how light behaves in three-dimensional spaces.

Because he was using the walls of existing buildings, the architect's main structural task was to build a roof to span the courtyard and turn it into an interior space. Boullée designed a roof with substantial wooden trusses (INSET) to do this job.

Boullée was fired with enthusiasm and did a whole series of drawings for the project, studies done with an artist's eye for light and shade. And no wonder: Boullée had wanted to be a painter but had been forced by his father to switch to architecture. A model of the library was exhibited to the public. Most of the responses were favourable. The scheme seemed likely to go ahead – more likely indeed than other grand plans for cultural buildings that were afoot at the time, such as proposals for a new opera house. With this support and the fact that the project was such a high-profile one, it is easy to see why Boullée would have been enthusiastic. But more than this, the architect liked the way in which his building could provide a fitting home for the great works of literature that had shaped French and European civilization.

As a Classicist, Boullée looked back to the ancient civilizations of Greece and Rome, and saw the links between them and modern Europe. One day, he found himself thinking about these links when looking at a print of Raphael's great fresco *The School of Athens*, in the Vatican. In Raphael's painting, groups of Greek philosophers talk and debate in a vast Classical interior, parts of which have huge, semicircular, vaulted ceilings. It struck Boullée that he could allude to this great tradition of learning by arranging some of the figures in one of his drawings of the library in a way that echoed Raphael's painting. By doing this, he was linking the learning of contemporary users of the library with those of the ancient world, and placing France and its library at the end of an illustrious tradition.

In spite of its quality, Boullée's reading room was never built. In 1789, the French Revolution came, banishing all thoughts of major building projects in central Paris. The library had to wait until 1854 before a substantial new building was put up to house the even larger collection that had mounted up by then. The library still preserves Boullée's drawings.

PANOPTICON

Jeremy Bentham and Willey Reveley, 1787

A Philosopher's Solution to the Question of Prison Design

'Morals reformed – health preserved – industry invigorated, instruction diffused – public burthens lightened – Economy seated, as it were, upon a rock – the gordian knot of the Poor-Laws are not cut, but untied – all by a simple idea in Architecture!' That was the prediction of the philosopher Jeremy Bentham. He was writing about the panopticon, a type of architectural design that would allow one person to observe a large number of people – without them knowing when they were being watched. So, at the end of the eighteenth century, the modern notion of surveillance was born.

Bentham's idea was not his own. As he frequently said, it was actually that of his brother, Samuel, who worked as an engineer and naval architect for Prince Potemkin in Russia and conceived the idea as a way of overseeing a large number of unskilled workers. Samuel's idea was that a supervisor would occupy a room in the centre of a circular building, with the workers ranged around him. When Samuel shared this idea with his brother Jeremy, the philosopher realized that it could work in a prison.

Prison conditions were a burning issue in late eighteenth-century Britain. Prisons were crowded, unpleasant, insanitary places and a spell inside was far more likely to result in disease and reoffending than in rehabilitation and a new start. Campaigners such as British reformer John Howard were attempting to change this, but they always ran up against the problem of money: prisons are costly to build and to run; prison reform usually meant more staff, making them costlier still. Bentham's idea was to design a circular prison in such a way that a single warder could keep an eye on a whole floor of prisoners.

The Benthams called their design the panopticon, from the Greek word meaning 'all-seeing' and the name of a giant in Greek mythology, Panoptes, who had a hundred eyes. The idea was simple. The prison inspector or warder sits in a room that Bentham called the lodge, in the middle of the round building.

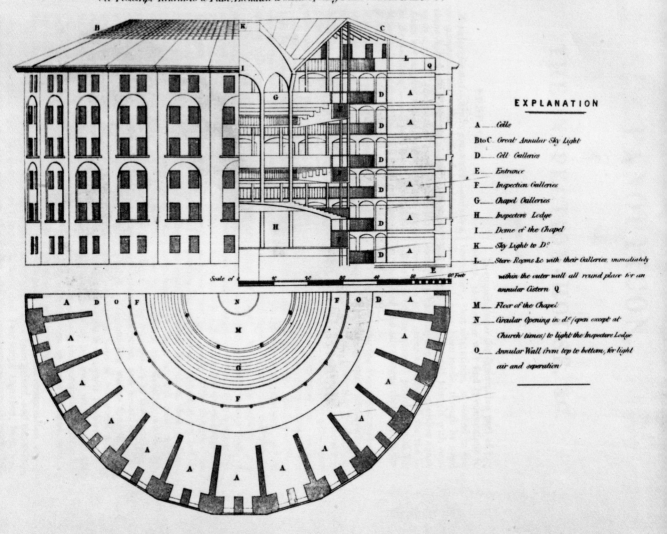

A General Idea of a PENITENTIARY PANOPTICON in an Improved, but as yet, Jan.ʸ 23.ᵈ 1791 Unfinished State

See Postscript References to Plan, Elevation & Section, being Plate referred to as N.º 2.

EXPLANATION

A___ Cells

B to C Great Annular Sky Light

D___ Cell Galleries

E___ Entrance

F___ Inspection Galleries

G___ Chapel Galleries

H___ Inspectors Lodge

I___ Dome of the Chapel

K___ Sky Light to D.º

L___ Store Rooms &c with their Galleries, immediately within the outer wall all round place for an annular Cistern Q

M___ Floor of the Chapel

N___ Circular Opening in d.º (open except at Church times) to light the Inspectors Lodge

O___ Annular Wall from top to bottom, for light air and separation

Scale of   10   20   30   40   50   60 Feet

Around the periphery is a series of cells for the inmates. A key idea of the plan is that, although the warder can see the prisoners, they cannot see the warder. Lights shine from the central area to the cells (which are fronted with iron grilles), helping the warder to see clearly. However, these lights dazzled the prisoners if they looked towards the lodge, and this, together with an arrangement of what Bentham called 'blinds and other contrivances', prevented them from seeing the warder. Therefore, although one person could not watch all of the cells at once, the prisoners could not see which were being

Willey Reveley's drawing combines an exterior elevation showing the plain outer walls with a cross-section revealing the inner structures of floors and cells, all visible from the central office or 'lodge'.

watched. This produced, in Bentham's words, 'the sentiment of a sort of omnipresence' – the prisoners acted as if the inspector could see everyone and so they were kept on their mettle, at a fraction of the cost of the normal complement of warders.

Another advantage that Bentham saw in his design was that the prisoners could be put to useful or profitable tasks. Prisoners at this time did not normally work – this was another activity that required close supervision and, therefore, cost money. With the panopticon system, it was argued, the surveillance was cheaper and work became viable. Bentham presented this as an economic advantage – his vision for the prison system involved government-backed private enterprise, paid for in part by the prisoners' labour. The jobs he proposed, such as walking on treadmills to power looms, was hardly the kind that would improve prison morale or prepare the inmate for life in the outside world.

Bentham thought that the panopticon idea had potential beyond the prison system. Why not have panopticon factories, schools or hospitals? But it was the prison idea that seemed most relevant to the needs of the times, and Bentham pursued it actively. He commissioned proper drawings from an architect, Willey Reveley, and wrote his ideas up in a book. Reveley was a young artist and architect. As a Classicist and follower of the great Georgian architect Sir William Chambers, he had been to Greece and drawn the monuments there. He seems to have been something of a dreamer of unbuilt dreams – among his schemes was a plan to straighten the River Thames, ironing out its bends in East London by rerouting the river across the Isle of Dogs.

However, Reveley's plans for the Panopticon were perfectly professional. They show a plain, six-storey building with no ornament but afford a certain grandeur by a series of semicircular relieving arches. Inside, the main floors each has some two dozen cells around the central lodge.

Bentham looked for a site where he could turn his idea into bricks and mortar. A number of places in London were proposed, but several proved problematic – usually because people with property nearby did not want a prison in their backyard. But, in 1799, a vacant site north of the Thames at Millbank was found, and Bentham bought it on behalf of the government for £12,000.

Then the scheme foundered. Adequate money for the building was not forthcoming, the government changed in

1803 and the new administration was less keen. Eventually, Bentham was paid £23,000 in compensation for his investment and efforts, and the plan was dropped. A prison was subsequently built on the site at Millbank, but it was not based on Bentham's principles or design. After the Millbank Penitentiary closed in 1890, the Tate Gallery (now Tate Britain) was built on the site.

Other prison designers adopted some of Bentham's principles, as did a few of the architects of Victorian workhouses in the nineteenth century. So, although Bentham's own Panopticon came to nothing, its influence lived on. Recent writers have also seen in it the origin of the ubiquitous surveillance that most city dwellers experience today. We, too, know that the watchers are out there, but, like Bentham's prisoners, we never quite know when their gaze is directed upon us.

CHAPTER 3
THE EXPLODING CITY

With the coming of industry, and America grew at a staggering pace.

Before the nineteenth century most of the world's population lived in the countryside and worked on the land. But after 1800 more and more people flocked to the cities to work in factories. London had a population of 1 million in 1800; this had risen to 6.7 million in 1900; the new town of Chicago had 300 people in 1830, 1.7 million by the end of that century. Such growth brought unprecedented challenges for builders, architects and everyone involved in local government. Houses had to be built rapidly – and the results were often substandard dwellings that condemned workers to live in squalid conditions, especially in cities such as London that had grown haphazardly out of densely planned ancient settlements. There were also enormous pressures on infrastructure, especially transportation systems and waste disposal. Unsanitary conditions put millions of families at risk from dread diseases such as cholera.

the cities of Europe

Some of the most ambitious schemes drawn up by nineteenth-century architects were attempts at addressing these problems. Britain, the first country to industrialize, produced many of the most outstanding. A quay and new drainage system, a vast circular complex combining road, railway and shops, a multi-storey cemetery in the form of a pyramid – these were just some of the proposals put forward to improve London. Other cities addressed different issues, from cultural provision in Washington DC to a project for a royal palace in Athens for the newly independent nation of Greece.

The diversity of these schemes is typical of their period. Some such as Joseph Paxton's startling Great Victorian Way are daringly modern, using an exposed iron framework, which was new technology in the middle of the nineteenth century. Others such as the enormous plan for an American National Gallery of History and Art in Washington are designed in revivalist styles – in this case in every historical style from ancient Babylonian to Roman. One, Robert Owen's plan for New Harmony, Indiana, emulates the ideals of earlier eras and offers a design for an entire town. They are all responses to specific needs, and all bring typical nineteenth-century inventiveness to bear, either stylistically or in terms of layout and planning. But many also point the way forward, to improvements in sanitation, conservation or museum provision, giving these very Victorian designs an enduring life and relevance.

NEW HARMONY

Thomas Stedman Whitwell, *c.*1825

Utopia on the Banks of the Wabash River

To set up one utopian settlement is a notable achievement. To set up two, on different continents, is a sign of true determination. This was the fate of Robert Owen, a British manufacturer and social reformer. Reacting against the laissez-faire economic policy of the time, Owen developed a form of utopian socialism that has been seen as a forerunner of the cooperative movement. His idea was to offer employment to the urban poor, settling them in new cooperative villages where they earned fair wages and had access to support in times of need. Although Owen's mills did well and he made a personal fortune, his business partners were unhappy with the reduced profits because of the cost of welfare. So he decided to make a new start in a new country. Owen travelled to North America in 1824 to create a 'New Moral World', a place where education would be provided, where workers would share in the profits of enterprise and where people would find happiness.

His chosen site was New Harmony, Indiana, a town that had been founded by the Harmonists, a group of German Lutherans, in 1814. However, they stayed only ten years, deciding in 1824 to move back to their original home in Pennsylvania. They sold their property in Indiana to Owen, who set about recruiting people to live and work there. He attracted many – although alongside those who were keen to work there were a number of people who hoped to sponge off the others. They soon had a population of 780 and Owen managed to get them to agree to a constitution based on the principle of equal rights and duties, and got the place working.

However, Owen felt that the community would function better in a purpose-built architectural setting. He began to work with an architect, Thomas Stedman Whitwell, on a plan to rebuild the town as an ideal city. It is not known why Owen chose Whitwell, an obscure provincial architect who had worked in the architectural office at London Docks and who does not seem to have produced any major buildings. It may have been their common interest in ideal communities.

OVERLEAF *This picture's high viewpoint shows the rectangular layout of the proposed town of New Harmony, the lawns inside and around the periphery, and the Wabash river in the background.*

In England, Whitwell had designed an ideal town, which he called Southville, to be built near Leamington Spa not far from his home town of Coventry. This scheme had been exhibited at the Royal Academy in London in 1819, and Owen might have seen the plans.

To create his ideal city, Whitwell went back to the classic authors who wrote about utopias – he cites Plato (author of *Republic*), Francis Bacon (*New Atlantis*) and Sir Thomas More (*Utopia*) as his inspiration. His planned city is square with corner towers and at first glance the design looks like one of the fortified ideal cities of the Renaissance. But in reality it is nothing like that. Surrounding the outer walls, where the moat would be, is a 100ft- (30m-) wide esplanade containing lawns and gardens, where people could take leisurely walks. The outer ranges of buildings, where the defensive walls would be in an earlier city, actually contain the housing; the four corner towers are schools (for 'infants, children and youths' in Whitwell's account) and an infirmary. The schools also

Reconstructed log cabins at New Harmony show the kind of buildings that were used by the original Harmonist settlers when they arrived in 1814–15 and that were there when Robert Owen purchased the town a decade later.

Robert Owen

have 'conversation rooms' for adults on the ground floor – an indication that some kind of improving activity for adults was also envisaged. Other buildings hold services such as kitchens, brewhouses and bakehouses, and there is ample provision of cultural buildings such as museums and libraries. At the centre is an imposing round building. This is not, as one might expect, a church – Owen's New Harmony was to be a secular community – but a conservatory housing exotic plants. Green space was important to Owen, and there are large expanses of garden and lawn between all the buildings.

It was very impressive, and it was more than a rapid application of some ideas from Bacon and Plato with input from an idealistic social reformer. Whitwell actually visited New Harmony, saw the site and met the people. This gave him a major stake in the scheme, and he published it in a pamphlet in 1830 – a move that was no doubt both an attempt to convince members of the New Harmony community and an ambitious bid for recognition by an architect who had not produced any major buildings.

But, by this time, it was becoming clear that the project had little chance of turning into bricks and mortar. The New Harmony residents were not unified. Some continued to follow Owen's principles, some started disputes about the way the town was run, while others left for another new start elsewhere. However, New Harmony did not disintegrate completely and did foster some remarkable achievements. Owen's eldest son, Robert Dale Owen, was a teacher and social reformer, an abolitionist who also campaigned for women's rights and free public education. There was also a strong contingent of scientists and teachers in the town, thanks mainly to Owen's colleague William Maclure, who was president of the Academy of Natural Sciences in Philadelphia. Maclure attracted other scientists and scholars to New Harmony, and Robert Owen's third son, David, was a noted geologist. A number of important books on geology, entomology and other scientific subjects were produced at New Harmony's printing press in the nineteenth century. The town's architectural legacy was not the one Owen and Whitwell hoped for, but the cultural legacy was valuable.

As for Whitwell himself, he seems destined to be remembered for his disappointments, the failure of his projects for Southville and New Harmony especially. His career ended in tragedy. The Brunswick Theatre in London, one of his biggest completed designs, suffered a roof collapse three days after it opened. A number of people were killed and Whitwell was blamed, although he insisted that the disaster was caused by theatrical machinery being hung on iron roofing beams that were not designed for the additional load. Whatever the cause, he seems to have designed little after this tragedy, apart from a prison in Coventry.

PYRAMIDAL CEMETERY

Thomas Willson, *c.*1831

A Multi-storey Solution to the Overcrowding in London's Cemeteries

By the 1820s, major British cities were beginning a rapid rise in population that only accelerated as the nineteenth century went on. The success of British industry, combined with the wealth coming in from an expanding empire, ensured this growth. Because London was a cramped and chaotic city, the amount of space for the most basic facilities was limited and even the cemeteries were overcrowded. In fact, the dead were not just buried close together, but also laid on top of one another, to a point where the ground level in churchyards began to rise alarmingly.

Far-sighted architects and planners had been raising this issue for centuries. After the Great Fire of London in 1666, Christopher Wren had suggested making provision for burials in the countryside just outside the city. However, contemporaries thought such proposals were unnecessary. London made do, until a crisis point was reached in the 1820s, when the graveyards were at bursting point and there was also a serious hygiene risk.

Various people came up with proposals, mostly along the lines of large cemeteries in open spaces on the edges of the city. But one man offered a radical solution. Thomas Willson's idea of the early 1830s was for an enormous pyramid, built on open ground available on Primrose Hill, north London, a site that had already been proposed for a conventional cemetery. The pyramid was to cover 18 acres (7.3ha) of land and rise to ninety-four storeys. As Willson argued, those 18 acres (7.3ha), 'being multiplied by the several stages to be erected one above the other will generate nearly 1,000 acres [405ha], self-created out of the void space overhead as the building progresses above the earth'. The structure would hold, Willson estimated, some 5 million corpses, solving London's burial problem at a stroke. He formed a company to promote the idea.

The cemetery would have made a massive impact on London's skyline. Primrose Hill is a prominent green space overlooking the centre of the city and to place on it a pyramid

THE PYRAMID.

TO CONTAIN FIVE MILLIONS OF INDIVIDUALS.

DESIGNED FOR THE CENTRE OF THE GENERAL CEMETERY OF THE METROPOLIS.

with an apex higher than the dome of St Paul's Cathedral (then London's tallest building) would have transformed the appearance of the capital. It seems an odd idea now, and must have been bizarre in 1831.

However, the notion of building a cemetery in the form of a great pyramid was in some ways a timely one. Willson's idea came to him at a point when ancient Egypt and its antiquities had become fashionable. This had happened largely because of

Thomas Willson's cross-section of the pyramid includes in the foreground a large-scale version of a small part of the structure, so that the network of thousands of vaults is clear.

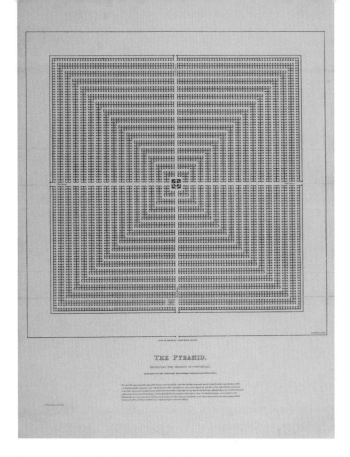

THE PYRAMID.

On the ground floor, fifteen concentric corridors give access to thousands of tombs. The same pattern is repeated, with progressively fewer corridors, on each upper storey.

the work of the Italian archaeologist and adventurer Giovanni Belzoni. Belzoni, who had had a chequered career as engineer, would-be monk, barber and circus strong-man, settled in England in 1803 but travelled widely with the circus. Contacts made on these travels eventually led him to Egypt, where he wanted to demonstrate a device he had invented for raising the waters of the Nile. Instead, he got a job working for Henry Salt, the British consul in Egypt, to remove a seven-tonne bust of Rameses II from Thebes – a challenging engineering job that he accomplished successfully, shipping the bust to London, where it still resides in the British Museum. In Egypt, Belzoni also cleared the temple of Abu Simbel of the encroaching sand, explored the second pyramid at Giza and opened the tomb of Seti I.

Belzoni published his findings when he returned to England, and in 1820–1 staged an exhibition containing a reproduction of Seti's tomb in the Egyptian Hall, an Egyptian-style museum in London's Piccadilly. Belzoni's publications and exhibition popularized the art and architecture of ancient Egypt, and many people discovered for the first time the importance of death in Egyptian culture. The stage was set for more Egyptian-revival buildings.

So Willson's giant pyramid was in line with the fashion, and the architect worked out the details, many of which are not apparent from the most widely known cross-section drawing, so that it might suit its setting and purpose. The structure is of brick but faced with tough, durable granite; a tall obelisk crowns the pyramid. There are four entrances and a central shaft for ventilation. Ramps enable bodies to be brought in with ease. Each vault or catacomb has room for twenty-four bodies. A chapel is naturally included, and accommodation for the keeper, sexton and superintendent are all part of the plans.

Willson worked out the finances, too. Parishes (or families) could acquire vaults at £50 a time. With a need to bury some 40,000 deceased per year, there would be a steady income. The total potential income would be enormous. Willson calculated that the proprietors of the pyramid could make up to £10 million, a staggering sum – according to some sources, roughly equivalent to £8 billion today. Investors in Willson's Pyramid General Cemetery Company were told to expect a return of 5 per cent per annum.

In spite of the figures and the spectacular architecture, the pyramid did not meet with the approval of the authorities, which preferred the traditional form of burial. So instead of Willson's plan they favoured a more conventional, ground-level scheme, and in 1832 Parliament passed a bill for setting up a 'General Cemetery for the Interment of the Dead in the Neighbourhood of the Metropolis'. It was effectively the end of Willson's scheme, and led in 1833 to the foundation of the burial ground at Kensal Green, a large cemetery based on Père-Lachaise in Paris. This was the first of a series of large burial grounds set up around London in the nineteenth century, from Highgate in the north to Nunhead in the south.

Willson revived the idea – as a 'Victoria Pyramid Necropolis' – twenty years later, but got no support. Kensal Green and its successors marked the end of Willson's proposal. However, the link between pyramids and mausolea has never quite gone away, and numerous small pyramidal tombs were built during the nineteenth century, some no doubt following the Egyptian fashion, some inspired by Willson's plans. In 1882, a design appeared for a proposed mausoleum for the US President James A. Garfield. The mausoleum was in the shape of a pyramid similar in proportions to the proposed one in London. The architect's name was Thomas Willson: he was probably Willson's son.

PALACE ON THE ACROPOLIS

Karl Friedrich Schinkel, 1834

A Vast Royal Residence Next to the Most Famous Ancient Monument in the World

The year 1833 marked the end of a long period of turmoil in Greece. The country had been under Ottoman Turkish rule since the fifteenth century, but in 1821 there was a revolution, followed by a long war of liberation. Greece was then briefly a republic, but the president, Ioánnis Kapodistrias, was assassinated in 1831. With the support of friendly European powers, Greece turned its back on republican government and became a monarchy and finally, in 1833, the Greeks elected the young Bavarian prince Otto von Wittelsbach as king. Otto, younger son of King Ludwig I of Bavaria, was chosen because he was the descendent of two ancient ruling dynasties of Greece. He arrived in the Greek capital, Nauplion, in triumph. He was just seventeen years old.

Plans were soon underway to relocate the capital to Athens, a city that was the centre of ancient Greek civilization and the obvious choice for a regime that wanted to make a new start while identifying itself with the country's Golden Age. In the early nineteenth century, Athens was a small town of around 10,000 inhabitants, and schemes were put in place to build the new facilities needed for a capital city. One essential was a royal palace, and several architects were invited to submit proposals. Principal among these was the great Prussian architect Karl Friedrich Schinkel (Otto was led to him via his family's links to the Prussian royal family). Schinkel's daring plan was to build the palace on the Acropolis, overlooking the city and right next to the greatest ancient Greek monument of all – the Parthenon.

Even in the 1830s, when respect for ancient sites was not on the same level as today, Schinkel's plan was colossally daring. He was completely redeveloping one of the most famous ancient sites in the world and, with still more chutzpah, was proposing to let his own Neoclassical architecture stand in close comparison with the temple where, for nineteenth-century historians and architects alike, it all began.

If anyone could get away with this, it was probably Schinkel. A noted Neoclassicist who drew inspiration from

Marble, rich paint finishes and gilded sculpture characterize Schinkel's designs for the palace interiors, as seen in this great hall.

ancient Greek (rather than Roman) architecture, he was director of the Prussian Office of Works and had already built many buildings in Berlin (such as the Neue Wache, the Altes Museum and the Schauspielhaus), helping to turn it into a worthy Prussian capital. It was not just a strong recommendation from the Bavarian royal family that made him an obvious architect for a high-profile project in Athens.

Stylistically, too, Schinkel seemed the right choice. He saw himself in a direct line that began in ancient Athens. His work was not, as it was with lesser architects, simply a matter of copying the Greek orders and applying them to his buildings. It was about combining plans that were effective in the modern world with the kind of beauty he found in Greek architecture. 'The principle of Greek architecture is to render construction beautiful', he writes, 'and this must remain the principle in its continuation.' It was natural, in a way, that the climax of his career should come in a building on the Acropolis itself.

Schinkel presented plans, elevations and perspectives of the palace. These drawings are strikingly beautiful, Schinkel having begun his career as a painter. They show a building that is big, but not vast, and one that sits impressively on the Acropolis. The main part of the palace complex is located at the eastern end of the site, and consists of a tightly planned series of reception rooms arranged around courtyards that offer shade, air and green space. There are also colonnades, providing more shade and air, as well as forming a dramatic columned facade looking out from the rock on the southern side.

The palace is a low-slung building of a single storey, arranged so that the Parthenon would not be totally dwarfed – the temple was taller than most of the new buildings and stood out from many viewpoints. The complex is designed to be entered via the ancient gateway, the Propilaia, which still stands at the western end of the site. From there, the entrance route takes one across the Acropolis, past a ceremonial courtyard in the form of an ancient hippodrome, beyond which is the ancient temple of the Erechtheion, with its famous porch held up by elegant caryatids. From here, the visitor would pass the ruined Parthenon to the palace itself.

Schinkel's design gave the Greek king much of what he wanted: a convenient, modern palace that was in a defensible position, and displaying strong links to tradition. However, it would have been expensive to build, and there were issues with the water supply. Schinkel specified a system of pumps and conduits to address this, but it was still felt to pose a

The palace was designed to harmonize with the adjacent buildings. For example, the portico (INSET) mirrors that of the nearby Parthenon, and is not as large, so does not overwhelm it. However, the idea of placing the palace on such a sensitive site is completely inappropriate from a modern, conservation-conscious viewpoint.

problem. And there was, as Classical scholar Mary Beard has pointed out, another increasingly strong argument against it. There was a growing body of opinion that wanted to preserve the Acropolis as an archaeological site rather than obliterating much of it under a new development. To build next to the Parthenon in this way would be, as architectural historians such as David Watkin have said, to relegate it to the role of a glorified garden ornament. So Schinkel's plans were abandoned, and the Greeks chose another site, Syntagma Square in the centre of Athens, where Friedrich von Gärtner's design for a brick-built royal palace was carried out between 1836 and 1843.

Schinkel was an influential architect, who produced major buildings in the Classical style, which later architects tried to emulate. He also published his drawings and those of his unbuilt projects, including the Athens palace and another palace he designed for the Russian royal family. So, in spite of the fact that he died in 1841, too soon to gain from the building boom that occurred as Germany industrialized later in the century, his work was much admired. From a modern perspective, people – especially those with an archaeological conscience – are apt to be a little dismissive of the Parthenon palace project. The slightly condescending judgment of his colleague Leo von Klenze (the 'charming Midsummer Night's dream of a great architect') is echoed by some historians. But many architects are also admiring, and slightly envious, of Schinkel's nerve.

THREE-LEVEL THAMES EMBANKMENT

John Martin, 1842

A Painter's Forward-Looking Scheme for a Grand Embankment and Sewerage System

John Martin was one of the most famous English painters of the first half of the nineteenth century. His vivid canvases of Romantic landscapes, images of apocalypse and biblical scenes such as *Belshazzar's Feast* and *The Destruction of Sodom and Gomorrah* are arresting, colourful and very large. The general public liked his work, Prince Albert and the Tsar of Russia were among his admirers, and although critics tore into the melodrama and grandiosity of his paintings he remained a well-known figure and made a lot of money from selling prints of his work.

But John Martin was much more than a successful artist. He was deeply interested in science and technology and numbered men such as Michael Faraday among his friends. Martin, especially after his income from printmaking increased, was said to devote two-thirds of his time to engineering projects. The biggest of these – he called it his 'grand plan' – was a scheme developed in the late 1820s to build an embankment along the River Thames in London.

In the first decades of the nineteenth century, people were increasingly concerned about London's river. It was silting up, and because it served as London's main sewer it stank, and the smell increased as the population rose. As the river silted up, it looked likely to burst its banks and contaminate drinking water.

People did not yet know how infectious diseases were transmitted: they were concerned about the smell and were convinced that the feculent odour of the river carried a disease-bearing miasma (see entry on Split-Level City on page 30). There was, therefore, a flawed but powerful argument for getting the sewage away from human habitation and for embanking the river to prevent flooding. Cleaning the water and making the river deeper by containing it within its banks would also make it more navigable, answering another contemporary concern.

Martin attacked the problems on two fronts. First, he tackled the question of water supply: in 1828, he published *A Plan for Supplying Pure Water [to] the Cities of London and Westminster, and of Materially Improving and Beautifying the Western Parts of the Metropolis*. This suggested piping in clean water from a river northwest of London, so bypassing the wells and conduits currently used, which frequently yielded dirty and contaminated water.

The 'beautifying' aspect of the plan was particularly important to the painter. He proposed not only facilities such as bath houses but also waterfalls, fountains and ponds in the city's parks and gardens. These, said Martin, 'would add much to the beauty of the western end [of the city], and much to the comfort of thousands, and to the salubrity of the air'. Contemporaries were impressed. The *Literary Gazette*, for example, approved, while noting that the high cost of the scheme would probably put the authorities off.

The monumental architecture of John Martin's 1841 painting Pandemonium *gives an idea of the kind of structures the artist envisaged for his ambitious Thames embankment plan.*

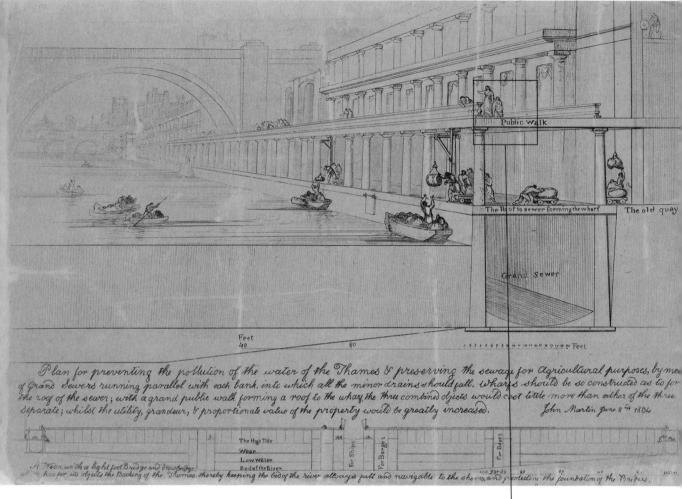

Plan for preventing the pollution of the water of the Thames & preserving the sewage for agricultural purposes, by means of Grand Sewers running parallel with each bank, into which all the minor drains should fall. Wharfs should be so constructed as to form the roof of the sewer; with a grand public walk forming a roof to the wharf the three combined objects would cost little more than either of the three separate; whilst the utility, grandeur, & proportionate value of the property would be greatly increased. John Martin June 2nd 1834

A Weir, with a light foot Bridge and drawbridge, has for its objects the Backing of the Thames, thereby keeping the bed of the river always full and navigable to the shores, and protecting the foundation of the Bridges.

Next, Martin had presented his ideas for the Thames itself. He published the first version of these in 1828, with a further, expanded, edition in 1832 and a final version of the plan in 1842. In this 1842 version, he proposes an embankment built up on three colonnaded levels, running for 4 miles 200 yards (about 6.6km) on the left bank and for a slightly shorter distance on the right. This would have created a grand vista of very plain Doric columns on either side of the river. Boats could moor by the embankment, which would be fitted with hoists for loading and unloading. The arcade under the columns provided shelter for people and goods. This was a scheme on an awesome scale, and might have created a riverside scene as grandiose as the dramatic if stagey architecture in the artist's paintings.

The real ingenuity of the scheme, however, is largely hidden from view. Beneath the embankment, running parallel with the river, is an enclosed sewer, paved with bricks and roofed

Above the Grand Sewer, Martin imagined a quay and a public walk (INSET) – the scheme served equally the hygienic, mercantile and civic spheres.

with sheet-iron held on iron arches that are also strong enough to support the quay above. The sewer is some 20ft (6m) wide and 20ft (6m) high.

Martin devised an innovative system for filtering the sewage, so that harmless water could be let into the river. This consists of a pair of large settling tanks – or 'grand receptacles' as Martin called them – in which the waste matter sank to the bottom. What Martin describes as 'the valuable manure which is at present wasted by being conveyed into the river' could be removed from the tanks and loaded on to soil boats that could moor nearby. The clean water that separated from the waste is allowed to flow through outlets towards the top of the tanks, and is let back into the Thames. There are clever traps, which work in a similar way to the curving outlet pipe in a modern lavatory, to prevent smells escaping from the tanks.

John Martin spent a lot of time and money developing and publishing his plans, and they were taken seriously when he appeared before the Parliamentary Select Committee on Sewers to explain them. If they had been taken up in the early 1830s they would probably have prevented many cholera outbreaks and saved numerous lives. But the authorities – ignorant of the true cause of cholera, and mindful of the need to save money – decided to muddle along with the system they had inherited, pouring untreated waste into the Thames very much as their ancestors had.

London had to wait another thirty-odd years for real change, after the hot summer of 1858 caused the 'Great Stink', affecting even the Members sitting in the Houses of Parliament. This time, the more comprehensive sewerage scheme of the engineer Joseph Bazalgette was adopted, transforming London for the good. By then, John Martin had died of a stroke, to be remembered more for his awe-inspiring and visionary paintings than for his equally dramatic and visionary plan to make Britain's capital clean.

LONDON, UK
GREAT VICTORIAN WAY

Joseph Paxton, 1855

A Glass-Roofed Street and Railway on a Supersize Scale

During the first half of the nineteenth century, London became the world's largest city. The capital of a vast empire, a port of global importance and the home of countless trading and manufacturing businesses, it had a population of 2.5 million by 1851, and was growing every year. Increasing numbers commuted to work. According to one estimate, 200,000 people arrived into the city on foot alone; further hoards arrived by train or omnibus. All this caused a huge traffic problem. There was congestion everywhere. People said it took as long to travel by road from Paddington to Waterloo as it did to go by train from Waterloo to Brighton. Major events such as the 1851

Although the Great Victorian Way had a structure like a greenhouse, the shop interiors were luxuriously decorated, offering a comfortable environment for shopping.

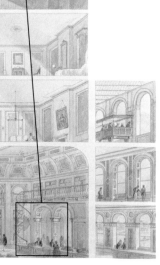

Great Exhibition, with its influx of millions of visitors, made
the traffic jams worse.

The Great Exhibition had succeeded in part because it
was housed in the Crystal Palace, an innovative prefabricated
building of iron and glass designed by the engineer Joseph
Paxton. Paxton was a remarkable figure. He began his
working life as a gardener and developed a passion for
designing larger and larger greenhouses, turning himself into
an authority on glass and iron structures in the process. The
Crystal Palace was the largest such building ever constructed.
Paxton now thought that he could solve London's transport
problems with an audacious plan based on a similar, and even
larger, glass and iron structure.

Paxton's idea was to build a circular covered way, a
combination of street, shopping arcade and railway, running
all the way around the centre of the city, in an 11 mile (17.7km)
circuit stretching from Moorgate to Victoria and back. The
structure would be of iron and glass, which meant that, like the
Crystal Palace, it could be made of prefabricated components
that could be produced off site and delivered as they were
needed to the builders. At the heart of the structure is a wide
street sheltered by a glass ceiling 108ft (33m) high. On each
side there is an arcade with shops and rooms above for storage
or apartments.

Beyond the shops is a railway, which Paxton proposed
should be on two levels – one for stopping trains, one for
expresses – allowing passengers to make short journeys or to
get right across the city with ease and speed. Where it passed

*Paxton's hugely popular Crystal
Palace demonstrated the potential
of the iron and glass construction
that he proposed using for the
Great Victorian Way.*

through residential areas, as in west London, Paxton suggested replacing the shops lining the way with housing, for which he also supplied plans.

The engineer called his structure the Great Victorian Way, in honour of the sovereign, and produced a map showing the proposed route. Its great loop around London passes and links all the major railway termini (Waterloo, Victoria, Paddington, Marylebone, Euston and King's Cross), following a path similar in some ways to the modern Circle Line, but including a stretch south of the Thames and adding a branch to link Piccadilly Circus with Waterloo.

Such was the optimism of the mid-Victorian period, and so great was the pressure on London's transport network, that Paxton's grandiose ideas were taken seriously. In 1855, he presented the plan to a Select Committee of the House of Commons that was charged with enquiring into communications in London. The scheme was well received. Both the queen and the Prince Consort were enthusiastic, too.

The transport provision alone made the Great Victorian Way appealing. But there were several other benefits. The amount of horse traffic in London made the streets unbearably dirty. Conditions were difficult for foot passengers, especially women in long dresses. Shopping could be an ordeal of dodging showers, avoiding horses, sidestepping smelly obstacles and watching that your purse or pocket was not being picked. The scheme could not eliminate all of this, but the additional railways promised to reduce horse traffic, and the covered way made life more pleasant for foot passengers, offering both more space and protection from the weather. Paxton suggested that it might even be possible to heat the way, making it warm in the winter.

The structure was also easy to maintain. Glass roofs were washed down by the rain and Paxton proposed cladding the exterior with ceramic tiles – an increasingly popular material in Victorian cities – which had similar 'self-cleaning' properties. The railway was dual-purpose, carrying passengers by day and goods by night, so serving another pressing need.

The greatest problem was the cost. Paxton estimated the price tag at about £34 million. This is a huge amount – estimates of today's equivalent hover around the £3 billion mark (i.e. £3,000,000,000). Paxton thought this could be raised through taxation or private investment – he was opposed to charging people to use the trains or other facilities. He was

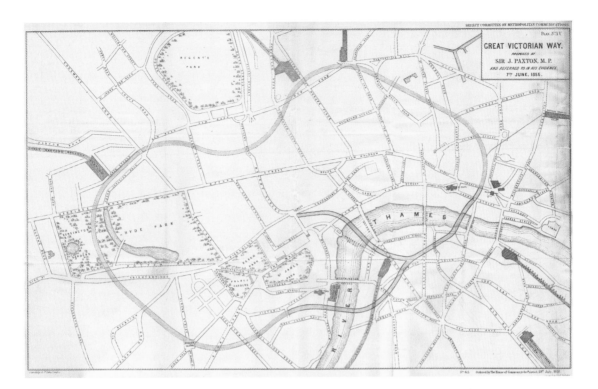

very persuasive. His engineering skills were tried and tested – everyone knew how successful the Crystal Palace had been. Now he was proposing a permanent scheme that would make London the greatest, most connected and most modern city in the world. With arguments such as this, even the immense cost seemed worth it.

However, the Select Committee that looked at Paxton's plans did not have the power to manage construction projects. So, in 1856, it set up another organization – the Metropolitan Board of Works – that would actually undertake engineering and building projects for the benefit of the city. But the Board had to wait years before its terms of reference and its budget were finalized.

By the time the Board was functioning, London had another, even more pressing problem: it needed proper sewers to alleviate the build-up of waste material in the River Thames. The rising population was making this problem worse every year, and the health risk was enormous. When the Board of Works did get going, this was the issue that was the most urgent. As a result, the Board's engineer, Joseph Bazalgette, was charged with creating a proper sewer network for London, and in the face of this equally major project Paxton's plans for the Great Victorian Way were shelved for ever.

Paxton's map shows the proposed route of the Great Victorian Way, looping around London from Hyde Park to the City. The scale of the scheme is similar to that of the Circle Line on the modern underground system.

LILLE CATHEDRAL

Cuthbert Brodrick, 1855

The Ultimate Gothic Cathedral?

In 1854, an architectural competition was announced in Lille, northern France. The town invited architects to submit designs for a new cathedral, and stipulated in some detail what they wanted: 'The style of the monument must recall the beautiful edifices, at once simple and imposing, of the first half of the thirteenth century. The church, of which the length is to be from 100 to 110m… must have one or two towers, surmounted by spires, three deeply recessed portals, a nave and two aisles, single transepts, a choir, a sanctuary, and apsidal chapels…'

Eighteen months later, a panel of judges met in Lille to consider the forty-one competition entries. The plans had come from all over Europe, with France and Britain (fifteen entries each) fielding the largest number of competitors. Among these were drawings by the British architect Cuthbert Brodrick, a little-known man from Hull, Yorkshire. Brodrick had risen to fame in 1852, when he won the competition to design Leeds town hall, a building nearing completion when the judges assembled in Lille. Leeds town hall is a Classical building of staggering monumentality, surrounded by an arcade of tall columns, with a tower ringed by more columns and topped with a dome; the masonry is tough northern British millstone grit.

The Lille design is very different from Leeds town hall, but also monumental and distinctive. Brodrick chose to have a single tower, topped with a spire that tapers to a height of 300ft (91m). The tower has a series of very tall, narrowly pointed windows and niches separated by slender shafts that recall the columns of the Leeds Tower – except of course that the style is totally different: where Leeds was Classical, Lille is Gothic. However, it was not quite the Gothic specified in the competition announcement: Brodrick chose to design the building in a slightly later form of the style, making the whole building more ornate – it was almost as if he was throwing a daring and rather arrogant challenge to the judges – my kind of Gothic architecture is better than yours.

The idea of a cathedral with a single tower and spire was also rather against the grain in France. Most of the great

OPPOSITE *Cuthbert Brodrick's drawing of the cathedral's west end shows a trio of entrance portals, as in the great medieval cathedrals of France. Further up are other typical Gothic features, including a rose window and rows of niches, with the crowning spire soaring above them.*

French cathedrals (Nôtre Dame in Paris, Amiens, Chartres, Laon, Rouen, Reims) have a pair of western towers. But a single-towered design is more at home in Belgium and the Netherlands, which are not far from Lille, set as it is in the far northern part of France. The required material – brick with stone dressings – is also fitting for the flatlands of northern Europe, although for the crypt Brodrick was allowed gritstone, a material with which, after Leeds, he would have felt at home.

Brodrick's competition entry is now known mainly from two drawings: one of the west front and spire; and one of the building from the east, showing the rounded or apsidal east end required by the competition. It is certainly an impressive design. Everything about it, from the trio of pointed portals to the dozens of openings and niches, leads the eye upwards to the tower and spire. The proportions of the tower make it look rather slender – again sending the viewer's gaze heavenward – and the spire itself is highly ornate, with rings of niches circling it like crowns. It is a very assured design.

However, the judges gave the first prize to another British architect, William Burges, and Brodrick had to be content with one of the silver medals. The designs were submitted pseudonymously, and still bore their pseudonyms when they were exhibited in Lille after the results were announced. Brodrick's designs, identified with the word Spes (Latin for hope, anticipation, but also chance), caught the eye of many visitors to the exhibition. One of these visitors was a writer for the British magazine *The Ecclesiologist*, who reported on what he saw:

So far as a popular verdict would decide the question, this design – apparently an English one – would be chosen for the first prize by the people of Lille; of whom an admiring crowd was always to be seen around it. And as usual the popular verdict would be unfair; for the author of this showy plan, though by no means a contemptible artist, has made his drawings ad captandum, *and not in honest accordance with the conditions under which he was allowed to compete… the style – developed Pointed – is not that prescribed by the regulations.*

By using the words *ad captandum, The Ecclesiologist* is alluding to the Latin phrase ad *captandum vulgus*, to ensnare the masses. The magazine is accusing Brodrick of being a kind of architectural demagogue, giving the masses what they want. This is almost certainly wrong. Brodrick was more likely to

Brodrick's design for the east end of the cathedral is a forest of flying buttresses and upward-pointing pinnacles, all of which draw the eye towards the slender tower and spire.

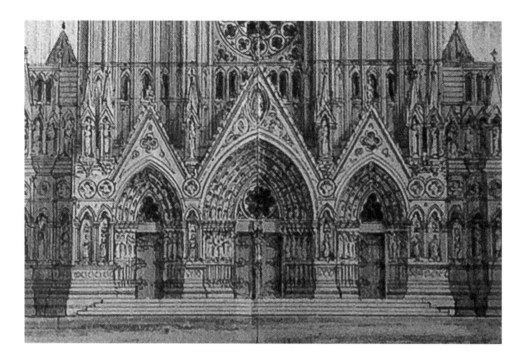

be trying to persuade the judges to think again, using his entry to convince them that his 'developed Pointed' style was better than the one required by their competition rules. It was an arrogant approach, and doomed to failure.

Although Burges won the competition, his cathedral was never built either. It seems that a design by an Englishman and a Protestant was too much for the authorities at Lille. They chose the plan by the highest placed Frenchman, Jean-Baptiste Lassus, an architect well known for his commitment to thirteenth-century French Gothic and for his close knowledge of French cathedrals, many of which he had restored. Lassus's design had been criticized strongly for being derivative, and being, as *The Ecclesiologist* puts it: 'a mere dead reproduction of the French style of 1200–1250'. But its very closeness to the old style made it attractive to the judges.

However, fate twisted again, and Lassus died in 1857. His design was modified by Charles Leroy, the local architect who took over after his death. Leroy designed by cribbing details from this cathedral and that, and adding them together in a hotchpotch. This, and slow progress on the work, meant that building remained incomplete for decades and lacked a west front until a final push was made in the 1990s, after which the church finally got cathedral status. By that time, Brodrick's design was known only to architectural historians.

Each of the three portals is crowned by a series of recessed arches decorated with sculptures.

Brodrick became a serial enterer of architectural competitions for high-profile buildings. In Leeds he did well, following the town hall with the unique oval Corn Exchange and the Mechanics Institute. The three buildings transformed the centre of the city. But he entered countless other competitions – for Preston, Bolton and Manchester town halls, for Liverpool and Manchester Exchanges, for the National Gallery and Whitehall government offices in London – and won none of them. Outside Leeds, he had to be content with minor architectural commissions. He was not so content and eventually retired to France where he is said to have painted, although little evidence has survived of any of his paintings.

Brodrick remains one of the great might-have-beens of architecture. His major buildings were Classical, and were designed on his own assertive terms. The designs for Lille Cathedral show that he could also produce work in the Gothic style, also on his own terms. It was a loss to architecture and to France that he was not given the chance to prove this and to please the people of Lille.

WATKIN'S TOWER

Sir Edward Watkin, *c.*1890

An Eiffel Tower for London

In the 1880s, Wembley was unknown to the world. As John Betjeman puts it, when describing northwest London in his famous film *Metro-Land*: 'Beyond Neasden there was an unimportant hamlet where for years the Metropolitan [Railway] didn't stop. Wembley. Slushy fields and grass farms. Then out of the mist arose Sir Edward Watkin's dream: an Eiffel Tower for London.'

Sir Edward Watkin, the man who hoped to put Wembley on the map with a new 'Eiffel Tower', was in many ways the typical successful Victorian businessman. Born in 1819 and son of a Manchester cotton merchant, he began his working life in the family firm but left to join a railway company. He did well and, by 1881, was a director of nine different railway companies, including London's Metropolitan, which ran northwest out of London and was the ancestor of the city's Metropolitan underground line. A Liberal Member of Parliament, he was also involved in campaigns for social good, as an early promoter of public parks and, like his father, a supporter of the Anti-Corn Law league that worked to repeal the laws that taxed wheat and pushed up the price of bread. This most energetic Victorian had two other burning ambitions: to build a tunnel beneath the English Channel, connecting Britain and France, and to construct a tower in London that would surpass the Eiffel Tower in Paris, which had been completed in 1889 and at the time was the tallest man-made structure in the world.

In the late 1880s, Watkin approached the engineer Gustave Eiffel, whose company had built the Parisian tower, offering him the chance to construct an even taller tower than the one in Paris – Watkin proposed a height of 1200ft (366m), almost 200ft (60m) taller than the Eiffel Tower. Eiffel turned down the offer, by all accounts because he thought it would be unpatriotic to be responsible for demoting his own tower to the second division. Watkin went ahead anyway, and organized a competition for a design.

A programme of entertainments for the park, held in July 1894 while the tower was being built, shows the structure as it would have appeared if it had been completed. The publicity was effective although the construction was not.

MONDAY, TUESDAY, WEDNESDAY, and FRIDAY,
July 16th, 17th, 18th, and 20th.

PRICE ONE PENNY.

Wembley Park.

PROGRAMME OF Music AND Entertainments.

(VIEW OF THE TOWER AS IT WILL APPEAR WHEN COMPLETED.)

TOTAL HEIGHT 1,150 FEET.

THE TOWER IN ITS PRESENT CONDITION

There were sixty-eight entries that ranged widely in their style and approach. Some were imitations of existing well-known landmarks – a copy of the Tower of Pisa or a homage to the Great Pyramid at Giza with accommodation for people who would grow food in built-in 'hanging gardens'. Others stuck closer to the Eiffel model, using a latticework of iron for the main structure. The latter approach was clearly what Watkin had intended, and the winning design by Stewart, McLaren and Dunn was along these lines. From a distance, the structure in the drawing looks like a scaled-up Eiffel Tower, but has eight legs rather than Eiffel's four. Closer to, it is clear there is more to it, with facilities on the upper floors such as restaurants, theatres, ballrooms, a ninety-room hotel and, near the top, a sanatorium in which patients could take advantage of the fresher, cleaner air. Turkish baths and an observatory are also part of the offering. It is like a vertical seaside pier, with added facilities.

This similarity to a pier was no accident, because Watkin had commercial motives as well as the wish to give London a major new monument. He not only hoped that the tower would be a money-spinner, but also that the people who would flock to visit it would get there using his Metropolitan Railway, recently extended northwestwards out of London. He hired one of the most prominent engineers of the time, Sir Benjamin Baker of Forth Bridge fame, to manage the construction.

The major setback was financing the project. Watkin hoped to raise funds by public subscription, but this produced

This drawing of the base of the tower under construction was published in The Graphic *in April 1894. The structure never got much higher than this.*

nowhere near enough money, so the company had to fall back on its own resources. The design was slimmed down – with a four-legged version of the tower – and construction work began in 1892. At the same time, Watkin commissioned a park to form a setting for the tower and an additional visitor attraction. This opened two years later and proved popular among Londoners as a place of escape from the noise and pollution of the city, even though the tower had not even reached first-floor level.

Work on the tower was slow because the builders hit structural problems. The change from eight to four legs altered the way in which the metalwork pressed on the ground, and even at this early stage of building structural movement started to occur. The first level, 154ft (47m) of iron latticework with a flat top, was done by 1895, but the subsidence was still causing problems and construction was called to a halt. After four years of further delays, the construction company went into liquidation with little further work done. Watkin died two years later, in 1901, as the Victorian era was coming to an end.

The park continued to thrive but the tower was a pathetic stump, which people took to calling 'Watkin's folly'. By 1907, the structure had been demolished with the help of high explosives. The park remained and became the site of the 1924 British Empire Exhibition and of the stadium that was to be the headquarters of British football. So Watkin's ambition of a great leisure facility at Wembley was fulfilled and Wembley became famous, though not in the way he imagined. A few other, shorter, British near-equivalents were built in the 1890s, though only the 518ft (158m) tower at Blackpool survives from this era of iron aspiration. Moreover, Gustave Eiffel's tower remained the tallest of its kind.

But Watkin had also started something else – he gave a kick-start to the idea of competing to produce the world's tallest building. The 1880s was the decade in which the first skyscrapers – tall office buildings with a structural iron frame – were built in Chicago. However, those first Chicago skyscrapers were not very tall by modern standards. The one generally said to be the first – the Home Insurance Building completed in 1885 – had just ten storeys and a height of 138ft (42m). The Eiffel Tower and Watkin's attempt to surpass it went far beyond that and paved the way for the race to build higher that gathered pace in the early decades of the next century. With ever-taller buildings, we are still seeing the effects today.

NATIONAL GALLERY OF ART AND HISTORY

Franklin Waldo Smith, 1891

A Complex of Buildings in Many Styles, from Babylonian to Gothic

'You are one hundred years ahead of your time.' That was the reaction of a contemporary to a set of proposals that appeared in the USA in 1891: a national gallery on a gargantuan scale, with buildings in the historical styles of the artefacts they contained, right in the centre of Washington DC. It was the vision of Franklin Waldo Smith, a Boston hardware manufacturer on a mission to improve life, education and culture in the USA. It is an extraordinary proposal, a collection of substantial buildings in eight different ancient styles, from Babylonian to Roman, fronted by a spacious court bounded by curving colonnades such as those in front of St Peter's, Rome.

An idea like this could come only from the mind of an exceptional man. Smith

Ancient Classical was just one of the many styles that Franklin W. Smith adopted for the National Gallery.

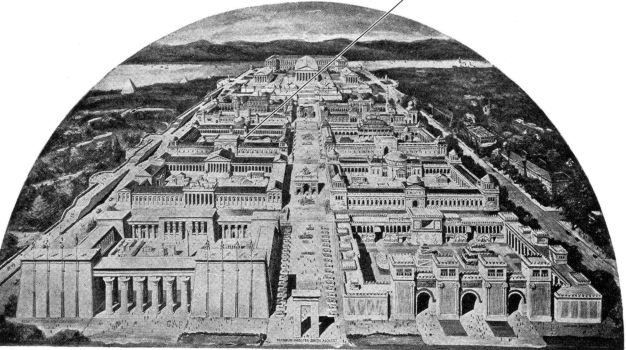

PAUL J. PELZ, HENRY IVES COBB, } Advisory Architects.   FRANKLIN WEBSTER SMITH, Architect.   HARRY DODGE JENKINS, Pinxit.

DESIGN FOR NATIONAL GALLERIES OF HISTORY AND ART.

was an entrepreneur who amassed a fortune building up a
business that supplied big clients such as the US Navy; he
became involved in a potentially ruinous dispute with the navy
that landed him with a prison sentence (Abraham Lincoln
intervened to save him); and he was a great promoter of
improving and utopian schemes. One of these was a plan to
start a new agricultural settlement in Tennessee, to offer a new
life to out-of-work factory employees. Another was his plan for
the National Gallery.

The idea started when Smith was on holiday. He travelled
widely in Europe, North Africa and the Middle East and
became fascinated by the ancient civilizations of these regions,
and especially their architecture. He also visited London's
Great Exhibition in 1851, again marvelling at the variety of arts
and crafts from all over the world.

As a way of keeping the remains of the Old World
civilizations in his mind, and of showing others what they were
like, Smith made detailed wooden models of them. This was
a rather bizarre pastime for a busy entrepreneur, but Smith
was convinced that reproductions of ancient buildings could
be educational. Museums containing models, he reasoned,
could enhance American towns and cities and help people
who could not travel to Europe understand past cultures. But
Smith wanted to go farther than small-scale wooden models
and took his interest to another level by commissioning life-
size reproductions or pastiches of ancient buildings. The first
was a house in Florida, the Villa Zorayda, built in the Moorish
style, in partial imitation of the Alhambra. Still more ambitious
was a recreation of a large Roman town house, which he
called Pompeia. Furnished in Roman style, with a mixture of
carefully made reproductions and objects he had collected in
Europe, it became a successful tourist attraction, bringing in
some 60,000 visitors in its first four years.

Smith was convinced that Pompeia could lead to something
far larger: a national museum on a truly American scale.
During his European travels, he took in the continent's great
museums and galleries, from the Vatican to London, Munich
to Paris. He noted their contents and compared them with
America's lack of similar public collections. Above all, he was
impressed with the newest addition to London's cultural scene
– the South Kensington Museum, later to become the Victoria
& Albert Museum, with its collections of decorative art and
design through the ages.

Begun using the profits made by the Great Exhibition of 1851, the South Kensington Museum was already building up a world-class collection as the curators made new purchases and private collectors contributed generous donations. It was expanding its premises to accommodate this material, and the government was supporting it with grants.

It seemed obvious to Smith that the USA should have something similar – but even bigger and better. He was pleased to find that others were having similar ideas. Reading *Travels in South Kensington*, a book by another American, M. D. Conway, he found a conversation between Conway and a member of the museum staff. Asking the curator if a similar museum would work in the USA, he received this response: 'Let them plant the thing and it can't help growing, and most likely beyond their powers – as it has been almost beyond ours – to keep up with it.'

Encouraged by such comments, Smith set to work planning the vast gallery and giving speeches promoting the idea. In 1890, the successful architect James Renwick Jr, who was working on a bell tower for the Cathedral of St Augustine, Florida, heard one of these speeches and offered his support. Over the next few months, Smith and Renwick pored over the plans. They worked out the arrangement of the buildings in terraces. They planned the galleries, proposing single-storey structures built economically out of concrete, which Smith argued was the best material for moulding the decorations for the various styles they planned to imitate. Beneath were basements containing workshops where models of ancient buildings, casts of sculptures and other artefacts could be made. Proposals were laid out for reconstructions of everything from an avenue of Egyptian sphinxes to the houses of Luther and Mozart. The whole complex was designed to be spacious, Smith being mindful of the way in which museums such as the V&A and Louvre had become overwhelmed with gifts and acquisitions.

The following year, Smith published a book outlining the proposal, giving the educational and prestige arguments for the museum, pinpointing a site by the Potomac River in central Washington, DC, indicating costs and presenting Renwick's plans and drawings. The book also laid out the 'hidden' benefits of the museum: educational work in the form of lectures and publications; the provision of historical information; the commissions it would generate for works such

as paintings of historical scenes; and the part it would play in educating people involved in the applied and decorative arts. Smith and Renwick had 5,000 copies printed and began to tour the country gathering more supporters.

There was plenty of backing. Newspapers all over the USA published supportive articles. Senators praised the project. Teachers and scholars were enthusiastic. But the timing was not right. The year 1893 was a bad one for the US economy and the recession lasted for several years. There was a flurry of interest again *c.*1900, when Smith opened a smaller-scale museum in Washington DC, called Halls of the Ancients, full of models of buildings from the ancient world and with an entrance based on the hypostyle hall of the temple at Karnak, Egypt. However, Smith fell on hard times after a break-up with his wife and died in poverty, his dreams unrealized. Although the museums of the Smithsonian Institution now fulfil many of Smith's goals, the visionary National Gallery was never built and the Halls of the Ancients became a car park.

Smith built this house, called Pompeia, as an educational resource, to illustrate the life of first-century Rome. Although a passable imitation of a Roman nobleman's house, it is actually inspired by a novel, Edward Bulwer-Lytton's The Last Days of Pompeii.

CHAPTER 4
BUILD IT NEW

'Make it new' was the Modernist to his fellow writers in the early twentieth century.

But the call for the new did not end with poetry – in all the arts, the new century led to appeals for fresh approaches in tune with the times. In the visual arts, this was the era of successive and varied movements – Art Nouveau, Cubism, Futurism and Constructivism all exploded suddenly and dramatically at the end of the nineteenth century and the beginning of the twentieth. All of them had an effect on architecture, with architects eager to ditch the reliance of the revival of old styles that had dominated the Victorian era and come up with something radically different.

One way of being modern was to embrace modern technology. The Futurist city designs by the Italian architect Antonio de Sant'Elia are built around modern transportation routes – there seems to be more room for railways and cars than for people, a feature that is typical of the Futurists' obsession with machinery and speed. Vladimir Tatlin's Monument to the Third International is modern in a different way – a structure

poet Ezra Pound's appeal

that uses metal and motors to make it move like a giant mobile, to create a vivid symbol of revolution. Cubist architecture, by contrast, all odd angles and crystalline shapes, conceals its structure but must have looked no less strikingly new.

Some of these structures were more about sculpting interesting forms than producing practical buildings. The Cubist house in Paris is an example – although if Cubist architecture had caught on in Paris (as it did, briefly, in Prague) its dramatic shapes might have ushered in Art Deco a decade earlier. Erich Mendelsohn's designs for Pleasure Pavilions – effectively, Expressionist designs for large, inhabitable concrete sculptures, some looking like elaborate seashells, others like sails – are further examples. They linger in the mind, but architects did not learn to be so sculptural with concrete until some forty years later.

In many ways, the shockingly new buildings that had most to teach later designers were the skyscrapers. Whether it was the Catalan Antoni Gaudí assigning a tall hotel as a series of curves, Ludwig Mies van der Rohe cladding a tower from top to toe in glass or Eliel Saarinen pioneering the classic set-back form of the American skyscraper, all predicted design trends that were taken up later, transforming cities worldwide.

CONCERT HALL FOR THE INTERNATIONAL EXHIBITION

Charles Rennie Mackintosh, 1898

A Hundred Years before the Millennium: A Great Dome for Glasgow

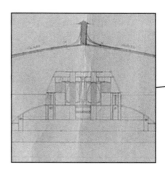

In the late 1890s, Glaswegians were excited to learn that their city was going to host a big international exhibition. Large exhibitions or 'world's fairs' were major events, and a successful event could benefit a city hugely – in income, job creation and general prestige. Glasgow had staged an international exhibition in 1888, and one result of this was funds towards the building of the city's municipal art gallery in Kelvingrove Park. Such spectacles were also good news for architects – there would be buildings to design – and although these were often temporary structures they would be large, high-profile projects. So when, in 1898, a competition was announced for designs for buildings for the coming exhibition, there was a great deal of interest, especially among architects in Glasgow.

One practice that was keen to enter was John Honeyman and Keppie, a successful firm of architects which had entered designs in the competition for the 1888 exhibition, but had not won. However, things had changed in the office since then. In 1889, they took on a new young draughtsman who turned out to be their most talented designer. His name was Charles Rennie Mackintosh.

Honeyman and Keppie was a good firm for a young architect to join. John Honeyman, who had been the creative force, was doing less work as he got older; John Keppie was the safe pair of hands who could manage projects and money, but was not a great designer. There was a gap to be filled, and, by the late 1890s, Mackintosh had risen from working as a humble draughtsman to being recognized as the most creative member of the team. He was embarking on his first commission for Kate Cranston, proprietor of a number of Glasgow tearooms that would eventually get famous Mackintosh interiors. Mackintosh had also begun work on some of his largest projects such as the Glasgow Herald Building and his masterpiece – the Glasgow School of Art. It was a good point

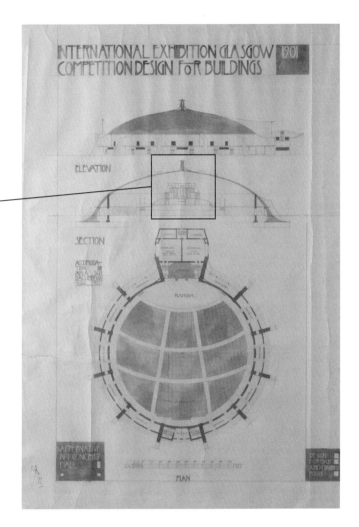

The plan of the round concert hall shows the walls with their large buttresses, and the protruding backstage area. The elaborate organ case behind the platform (INSET) can be seen in the architect's section drawing.

in his career to take on the plans for a big exhibition site. The brief called for several designs: an Industrial Hall for the main exhibition displays; a linked Machine Hall for an engineering exhibition; cafés and refreshment rooms; and a large concert hall – the grand hall – seating up to 4000 people. It was Mackintosh's design for the concert hall that showed his originality and flair.

The competition had a difficult start. Architects immediately noticed that the fee offered was below the usual percentage. The standard rate recommended by the Royal Institute of British Architects was 5 per cent of the costs; the Glasgow authorities were offering only 3 per cent. There were objections, but the organizers would not move. Even so, fourteen firms submitted plans.

For many of them, although the Industrial Hall was a major landmark, the concert hall was the key building. This was

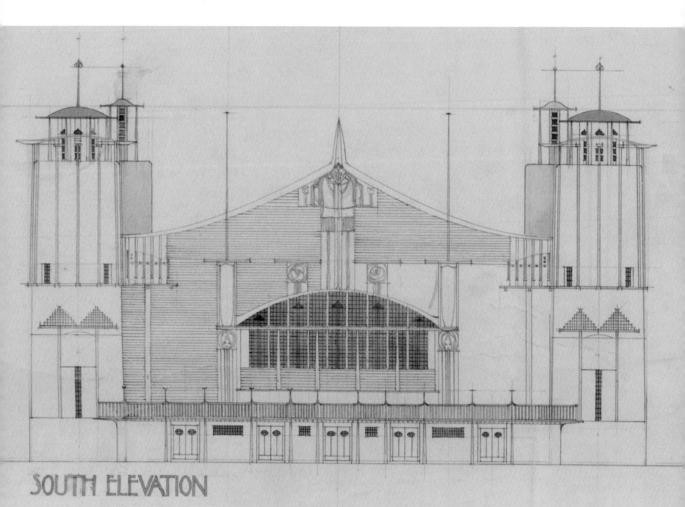

SOUTH ELEVATION

because the organizers asked for two alternative designs and also because there was a good chance it would be a permanent building, whereas the other structures would be taken down at the end of the exhibition. Mackintosh's Industrial Hall follows the expected pattern: a glass-roofed structure with a central dome and some octagonal towers. He also took a fairly conventional approach for his first design for the concert hall, which was an oblong building with corner towers.

The stand-out design was his second concert hall – a circular building with a daringly thin roof. Mackintosh designed a very shallow dome resting on metal roof trusses supported by twelve massive buttresses around the perimeter wall. Between each pair of buttresses is a vestibule, with only the main entrance emphasized by a grand portal. There is just one break in the great sweep of portals and buttresses – a protruding section that accommodates the backstage area; otherwise, the building is a perfect circle.

Mackintosh's designs for other buildings for the exhibition were move conventional, with the rectangular plans, tall corner towers, and ornate facades that the event's organisers would have expected. They also show the architect's very individualistic style of decoration, featuring slender pinnacles and use of the stylised rose motif.

We do not know a great deal about Mackintosh's design. On the surviving drawing, the architect does not specify the materials, but the roof trusses are drawn with rivets, so must have been either iron or steel – the use of metal roof trusses was common by this time and Mackintosh used steel widely in his buildings. The roof shell is very thin and so may also have been metal, but Mackintosh indicated that the centre part was to be glazed. This shallow dome spans a large auditorium without needing internal columns that might have blocked the audience's view. The architect noted the total seating capacity to be 4221, with 600 in a gallery, the rest on the ground floor.

What is clear from the drawing is how different Mackintosh's design was from other buildings of the time. It is not the circular plan – two other competition entrants put in round or elliptical designs for the concert hall – but the fact that no one had ever built such a large, shallow dome. Its shape recalls that of the domes of Byzantine churches. The largest Byzantine church, the sixth-century Hagia Sophia in Istanbul, has a dome 102ft (31m) across; the inner diameter of the dome of London's St Paul's Cathedral is a similar size. Mackintosh's dome is 180ft (55m) in diameter and shallower than its predecessors. It was a bold concept, and we have to look to much more recent buildings such as London's Millennium Dome to find something of similar shape, though structurally very different.

By the closing date for the competition on 15 August 1898, fourteen sets of drawings had been received. The judges made their decision the following month. The first prize went to James Miller. Mackintosh's designs did not even make third place. Mackintosh had to be content with designing some temporary exhibition pavilions for several companies, and for the Glasgow School of Art. The reason Mackintosh's design did not even come in the top three is probably the daring nature of the dome and the rather plain facades of the other buildings. The organizers wanted something they felt safer with. Mackintosh always did well with clients with less conventional tastes – such as the Glasgow School of Art and 'artistic' patrons such as Kate Cranston and the owners of some of his houses. The organizers of Glasgow's International Exhibition marched to a different drum.

HOTEL ATTRACTION

Antoni Gaudí, 1908

Curves Come to Manhattan

In Western architecture, most buildings are rectangular or at least have a plan based on the right angle. New York, like nearly every American city, is planned on a grid, with rectangular blocks, and this reinforces the power of the right angle, throughout the city. Occasionally, architects try to break out of this straitjacket and propose a non-rectangular building. Two of New York's most famous examples are Frank Lloyd Wright's Guggenheim Museum, with its spiral, shell-like structure, and Daniel Burnham's Flatiron Building, a triangular tower on a plot shaped that way because of the angle at which Broadway slices across the grid. Probably, the most dramatic of all these nonconformist designs was by the Catalan architect Antoni Gaudí, who drew up plans for a tall hotel with curving walls and towers, in 1908. The suggested site was in Lower Manhattan, near where the Twin Towers of the World Trade Centre were built much later.

Gaudí worked mostly in Spain, where, in Barcelona especially, he developed his style of highly distinctive architecture, a blend of curving walls, parabolic towers, eccentric ornament with little or no historical precedent, and catenary arches (the kind of curving arches that look like parabolas but in fact are based on the shape a rope or chain makes when hanging supported at both ends). It was a style that owed something to the Art Nouveau movement of the turn of the twentieth century, yet was completely Gaudí's own.

In 1908, two American businessmen approached Gaudí, asking for a design for a hotel – and the curvaceous Hotel Attraction was the result. It is a very mysterious project because the identities of the two men who commissioned it are unknown, although one of them was rumoured to be William Gibbs McAdoo, president of the New York and New Jersey Railroad Company and later Treasury secretary. The design then disappeared until the drawings were found by Joan Matamala i Flotats, a sculptor who had worked on the Sagrada Familia and was the son of Llorenç Matamala, one of Gaudí's closest collaborators. A number of the drawings were by

OPPOSITE *The hotel's curving geometry is quite unlike anything else in New York City. However, anyone familiar with Gaudí's great church of the Sagrada Família in Barcelona, with its groups of round tapering towers, will immediately recognize the style of its individualistic architect.*

Llorenç Matamala and when Joan Matamala published them in a book in 1956 some people thought that the whole story was a hoax.

However, some of the drawings are signed by Gaudí, and they display features typical of his work, such as the parabolic towers and catenary arches. They seem to be genuine. The building certainly looks like a Gaudí project. At its centre is a parabolic tower designed to be 984ft (300m) in height – it would have been the USA's tallest building in 1908. Adjoining it are several lower, dome-topped towers of various heights. The profile of the structure recalls in many ways the architect's famous great church of the Sagrada Familia in Barcelona, which has its own collection of unusually shaped spires. Instead of the cross finials that crown the spires of the Sagrada Familia, Hotel Attraction is topped with an enormous star.

Then there is the planned decoration. This is in Gaudí's usual style: a riot of colourful mosaic, glass and tile, some of it scavenged from the detritus of New York City, and much of it no doubt intended to be improvised by the architect as the building went up, which was Gaudí's customary way of working. In its stunning decorative finish and its bid to break out of the rigid New York grid, the tower certainly displays Gaudí's bravura, and his capacity to think things through in a different way from everyone else. It would have been a

The surviving interior drawings include this one of a grand reception room. The space is dominated by catenary arches supporting a curvaceous vaulted ceiling.

building that stopped people
in their tracks and made a
transformative impact on New
York's skyline.

Inside, it is if anything even
more surprising. As well as the
usual complement of luxury
bedrooms, there are public
spaces on a monumental
scale. The dining rooms are
enormous, and there are five of
them, one for each continent;
they could seat 2400 in total,
and are decorated with murals
illustrating mythological
subjects. There is a vast
theatre, where, in addition to
more Gaudí ornament, the
building's structure of steel
and reinforced concrete is
on display. In the upper part
of the tower are exhibition
rooms, including a cavernous
grand hall adorned with
statues of each of the US
presidents and a replica of the Statue of Liberty.

*This rapidly drawn cross-section
of the hotel shows the overall
shape of the towers, which rise
to several different heights, and
the enormous arches that Gaudí
envisaged for the lower levels.*

It is unknown why Hotel Attraction was not built. Theories
range from Gaudí's revulsion at the fact that the hotel could
be only for the rich, to illness and problems over the funding.
In a further twist of fate, the building actually failed to get off
the drawing board a second time. In the months after 9/11,
between late 2001 and early 2003, when New York was looking
for ideas for a building for the World Trade Centre site, a
number of Gaudí enthusiasts once more put forward the hotel
as a worthy successor to the fallen towers. The offer was not
taken up: a new design, specially conceived as a memorial to
those who perished that day, was more appropriate and timely,
so Gaudí's plans stayed in the archives. But whatever the true
story behind the building's design and its failure to get built in
1908, the plans remain a remarkable achievement, one of those
sideways leaps in New York architecture – like the three-sided
Flatiron Building or the spiralling Guggenheim Museum –
and a tribute to one of the great individualists of architecture.

MAISON CUBISTE

Various, 1912

A House Inspired by Crystals and Cubist Painting

In the years before the First World War, Cubism turned European art inside out. Artists such as Pablo Picasso and Georges Braque rejected the traditional idea of creating an illusion of depth in their paintings, splitting images up into a series of flat areas or planes, each showing part of the subject from a slightly different angle, so that one painting in effect had several different viewpoints. This revolutionary development happened in Paris, where Picasso's *Les Demoiselles d'Avignon* (1907) was probably the first Cubist painting. French artists were joined in the capital by people from elsewhere in Europe – Picasso himself was from Barcelona and many artists from central Europe also came to Paris and became Cubists. The place was an artistic melting pot.

At around the same time, architects and designers in Paris and elsewhere were looking for ways of creating buildings that would be equally modern. Old styles such as Classicism and Gothic, endlessly rehashed in the nineteenth century, seemed irrelevant to the modern age. The Art Nouveau style, with its decoration based on natural forms and sinuous curves, had been one way forward, but was becoming old-fashioned by 1910. Where else could architects look for inspiration? Around 1910–11, a number of architects in Prague thought they had the answer. By this time, there were numerous Cubists in Prague (Czechs who had visited Paris and returned home fired up by the new movement). A Czech architect, Pavel Janák, was inspired by Cubist painting to look for a way of using its flat planes and divided surfaces in buildings; he saw similar patterns in crystals and prisms. In 1911, he published an essay, 'The prism and the pyramid', in which he proposed an architecture made up of crystalline planes. Soon, he and other Czech architects were designing Cubist buildings, with angular facades that look as if they are made of crystals, or prisms or origami in stone. A few of these buildings were constructed in Prague and other Czech cities.

The idea quickly got back to Paris. A number of artists, mostly Cubists, met regularly for discussions at the studios of

the sculptor Raymond Duchamp-Villon in Puteaux, a suburb of Paris. The group included Duchamp-Villon and his brother Marcel Duchamp, other French artists such as Fernand Léger and Robert Delaunay, plus figures from abroad such as the Czech artist František Kupka. All kinds of topics, from theatre to philosophy, were discussed at the group's meetings, and the members were especially preoccupied with applying the ideas behind the new art to other areas of life. Another member of the group was the designer André Mare, who collaborated

The model of the Maison Cubiste was designed with proportions that would harmonize with typical European city buildings, but with revolutionary angular ornament.

with Duchamp-Villon and others to make a large plaster model of a Cubist house, to form a centrepiece to the exhibition of the 1912 Paris Salon d'Automne.

The model is more than 10ft (3m) high and 33ft (10m) wide, and shows the building's street facade. It has triangular-headed windows topped with multifaceted angular canopies. There are balconies in front of the upper-floor windows with balusters, again in an angular style. In the middle is a doorway with an extraordinary crystalline canopy resembling icicles and above it, on the skyline, a matching pediment or gable in a similar triangular form. Nothing like it had been seen in Paris.

For Duchamp-Villon, the house was a design in keeping with the rhythms of modern life. In a letter he speaks of 'lines, planes, and synthetic volumes' balanced 'in rhythms analogous to those of the life surrounding us'. It was for him a perfectly

The House of the Black Madonna in Prague is one of the few surviving Cubist buildings. It is the work of the architect Josef Gočár.

natural way to design a house, and he believed that this style could be applied to houses and other buildings that would fit comfortably within existing city streets.

When the outsize model was exhibited at the Salon d'Automne (and later at the 1913 Armory Show in New York) it did not strike visitors as so natural. Most people had never seen anything like it before, and it caused a stir. It did not draw on the past for ornament or style, and in this way it seemed to represent a clear break with the previous century. However, it is symmetrical and the overall proportions are traditional. Behind the facade of this outsize model are two rooms, again traditionally proportioned, but hung with Cubist paintings.

In truth, the house was not as revolutionary as the paintings hung on its walls, but revolutionary or not it began to take hold in Prague and the other Czech lands, where a number of Cubist buildings survive. But it did not take root in the rest of Europe. This was mainly because the Parisian audience associated it with the rest of the Cubist art in the show, which was widely condemned as 'foreign' and bad. In France in 1912, nationalism was on the rise and anything seen as alien was viewed with suspicion. People began to think that war was not far away. It was not the time for a new style of architecture drawing on sources from outside France.

As a result, architectural Cubism failed to spread beyond the Czech lands, and even there it was limited to a relatively few buildings, mostly in large cities such as Prague or Brno. There were also Cubist interiors such as the bizarre Montmartre nightclub in Prague, in which motifs such as those on the Duchamp-Villon house facade appeared alongside reliefs and sculptures in the Cubist style. Czech designers such as Janák and Josef Gočár also developed Cubism in the applied arts, with Cubist furniture based on crystal-like forms, and ceramics decorated with stripes, zigzags and more crystalline shapes.

The Cubist vases and sofas of the Czech designers, made in the years just before 1914, seem to anticipate the dramatic shapes and angles that became fashionable when Art Deco design took hold more than ten years later. It may be, if designs such as Duchamp-Villon's Maison Cubiste had been accepted in Paris, that a decorative Cubism would have evolved in western Europe and Art Deco might have developed earlier – before 1920 – rather than in the late 1920s. As it was, the Maison Cubiste was forgotten after the Armory Show and became an interesting footnote in the history of architecture.

CITTÀ NUOVA

Antonio Sant'Elia, 1914

A Futurist City Prefiguring the Architecture of Blade Runner

The Italian architect Antonio Sant'Elia got little chance to construct anything at all. Starting out as a builder, he opened his architectural office in Milan in 1912, but went off to fight in the First World War when his country joined the war in 1915. He was killed in battle in 1916. Sant'Elia left behind a large collection of drawings, including many for an imaginary metropolis, the Città Nuova (New City), a city of tall buildings with dramatic setbacks, covered streets and rapid highways. It looks as if it is mostly made of steel and glass, and it is strikingly modern for 1914: a new city indeed. Although the city was never built, Sant'Elia's beautifully executed drawings have influenced generations of architects and inspired film-makers who wanted to evoke futuristic urban landscapes, from Fritz Lang's *Metropolis* (1927) onwards.

What was behind Sant'Elia's city design? First of all, Sant'Elia was a committed member of the Futurists, an artistic group founded in Italy that wanted to transform art and make it fit for the modern age. The Italian Futurists gathered around the poet Filippo Tommaso Marinetti, author of the *Futurist Manifesto*, which expresses the group's love of technology, speed, youth and, most disturbingly, violence. They would have nothing to do with the past and wanted to sweep it away – violently if necessary – and replace it with a world in which machines were key. They were also extreme nationalists.

The Futurists even produced a separate architectural manifesto, which was probably written by Sant'Elia. Taking its cue from Marinetti's Manifesto, it rejects the great buildings of former civilizations: 'We feel that we are no longer the men of the cathedrals and ancient moot halls, but men of the Grand Hotels, railroad stations, giant roads, colossal harbours, covered markets, glittering arcades, reconstruction areas and salutary slum clearances.' Instead of finding value in religion and its architecture, the guiding light comes from the world of machinery and industry: 'We must invent and rebuild our Futurist city like an immense and tumultuous shipyard, active,

Sant'Elia's drawing of the central railway station is full of sloping, buttress-like elements, with expanses of glass and much structural iron or steel on display. All of these features are typical of the architecture of the Città Nuova.

mobile and everywhere dynamic, and the Futurist house like a gigantic machine.'

An architect who wanted to build in new ways fitted easily into this aesthetic. Futurist architecture, said Sant'Elia, should be all about exposed, 'raw or bare' materials and bright, 'violently coloured' surfaces. In Futurist cities, buildings would be made of iron girders and sheets of glass produced in factories using machines (there was no place for the arts and crafts here), and aeroplanes, trains and cars would have priority over pedestrians. The Futurist city was an exciting but heartless place.

One can see some of this in Sant'Elia's drawings of the Città Nuova. The buildings are on a huge scale, mostly multi-storey and set back so that they make wedge shapes, letting light into the streets below them. All these structures are drawn with rigorous, hard-edged precision. People would enter the buildings using mechanical means – next to each skyscraper was an elevator tower, connected to it by a series of bridges. Sant'Elia was fascinated by the lines of bridges, which are among the most striking features of his designs, providing a foil to the upward-thrusting skyscrapers. Critics have noticed that he includes more bridges than are strictly necessary, regardless of the huge cost that actually building them would have entailed.

Pairs of skyscrapers are sometimes linked by arches, to create covered highways below, but these streets are not protective arcades such as those of Victorian cities, but streets along which cars could pass and tracks along which trams could travel at speed. In fact, Sant'Elia was an early enthusiast for separating forms of traffic in this way, with different levels and routes for cars, trams and pedestrians. Some Victorian designers had proposed this sort of separation, but by combining it with an outwardly modern style of architecture Sant'Elia was a true forerunner of the planners and architects of the 1950s and 1960s.

The architecture is very industrial. Sant'Elia's love of iron as a building material must have been influenced by what he saw around him in Milan, where he worked, and by his own unbuilt project for a new railway station in the city. Reinforced concrete was also being used widely at the time, but, like iron, it was usually hidden from view under a covering of carved

This atmospheric drawing for the Città Nuova shows the architect's fascination with bridges. These structures enabled him to link parts of a building, join one block to another and create a number of different access levels, one above an another.

decoration. In factories, however, metal beams and concrete structures were left exposed, and this 'honest' architecture, in which structure was not hidden behind ornament, was one source of inspiration for Sant'Elia. The elevator shafts probably come from industrial architecture, too: elevators were manufactured in Milan and widely used there in tall factories. As in American skyscraper architecture, glass was used more and more lavishly. The Città Nuova's station for aeroplanes and trains, presented in an outstanding drawing, features a dramatic sloping glass facade on a huge scale. It would have been a major building and a focal point for the city.

Another break from the past was in planning. The communal assembly places of traditional cities, such as squares, have disappeared from the Città Nuova. Instead, the communal spaces are the railway stations and airports – transport hubs dominated by machines. It takes time, looking at the drawings, to recognize how mere humans fit into this urban pattern.

So far, so Futurist. Yet there are things about Sant'Elia's city that have their roots in the old. The setbacks, although they are uniform, setting up a pattern of slopes and wedges across the city skyline, are based on those of skyscrapers that had already been proposed or built in New York City and also on recent designs for set-back buildings by French architects such as Henri Sauvage. The palette used by Sant'Elia was very restricted: there were none of the violent colours here that the Futurists demanded in their new, assertive architecture. It is as if Sant'Elia is already starting to modify his vision and move away from the violent and disturbing predictions of the Futurists.

After Sant'Elia died in 1916, aged just twenty-eight, the Città Nuova drawings were not forgotten. Most of them had been shown in 1914 at the exhibition of another forward-looking artistic group of which Sant'Elia was a member – the Nuove Tendenze. Architects noticed them, and the bold conception and modern look of the drawings held their attention: the city designs lived on to influence skyscraper builders and city planners. Architects still find something to admire in the dramatic forms of the buildings. They influenced another art form, too – films. The Città Nuova is an inspiring presence behind the sets of Fritz Lang's 1927 *Metropolis* and, through that film's influence, in Ridley Scott's 1992 *Blade Runner*, affecting different audiences in new ways.

MONUMENT TO THE THIRD INTERNATIONAL

Vladimir Tatlin, 1919

A Constructivist Image of the Communist Revolution

The Russian Revolution of 1917 was a momentous event, transforming Russia itself and beginning a series of changes that brought communism to large parts of Europe. Russian communists realized what a major development this was – they saw the work of revolution as global ('Workers of the world, unite') and the Russian Revolution as part of a worldwide class struggle. The Russian organization Comintern, also known as the Third International, had as its task the promotion of revolution worldwide and fostering the unity of the world's communist groups. Soon they were calling for a monument, not just for the 1917 Revolution but also to communist revolutions everywhere.

*One of Tatlin's drawings for the monument was featured on the cover of a publication about the tower, by Nikolai Punin. The metal-framed glass structures, such as the pyramid housing Comintern's executive, are visible (*INSET*) behind the tower's beams and struts.*

Most artists initially responded to the call with the usual kind of monument – a figurative design featuring a statue of a specific revolutionary figure. But Vladimir Tatlin, the artist, architect and engineer who was given the job of coordinating post-revolutionary monuments, wanted something different: a new kind of structure for the radically new kind of world that, people hoped, the revolution would usher in. Tatlin was a fascinating if shadowy figure. He started his working life as a merchant seaman and ship's carpenter, then switched to art, learning how to paint icons in Moscow. But, in 1913, he visited Paris, where he saw Picasso's early Cubist works and the trend towards abstraction. By the time of the 1917 Revolution, he was producing abstract paintings and sculptures. He was not trained as an architect, but was fascinated by all kinds of structures and was restlessly inventive. He was especially interested in flight, and made bird-like gliders as well as sculptures that looked as if they had been caught in mid-air. This unusual artist was bound to come up with an unusual monument to the Third International, something unlike any construction seen before: a structure, according to one critic, made of steel, glass and revolution.

Tatlin's Monument to the Third International, often known simply as Tatlin's Tower, is an enormous spiralling form made out of steel and glass. At some 1300ft (almost 400m) high, it would have dwarfed Paris's more conventional Eiffel Tower and been the world's tallest building. Its proposed location, straddling the River Neva in St Petersburg (called Petrograd in this period) against a backdrop of eighteenth-century buildings put up by the emperor Peter the Great, made blatantly obvious the way it confronted the old world with something entirely new.

The form of the tower is unique. It is based on a steel framework in which two helixes describe upward curves, getting tighter as they rise higher, and held together by straight steelwork that leant outwards. It gives an impression of dynamism but also strength, echoing in its combination of curves and angles the style of the Constructivist art that was becoming popular in the post-revolutionary period.

There is something assertive about the tower's sheer size and location, and there is a similar quality in the materials. Historians often talk about iron, steel and glass as 'modern' materials. By 1920, they were not very new, but it was still very unusual to see an exposed metal framework such as this, with every strut and brace openly displayed. Metal was an industrial material, made in factories, assembled by workers and usually hidden from view. It was a world away from stone, plaster and brick – the traditional visible materials of architecture – and the contrast Tatlin's metal tower made with the stucco-covered Classical buildings of St Petersburg could not have been greater. The tower was an image of modernity.

The tower's framework held four inner structures, each constructed as a perfect geometrical form, each designed to revolve at a different rate, making the monument a literal image of revolution. These structures were intended to house the headquarters of the Comintern. At the bottom is the biggest of these, a cube, containing Comintern's legislature; it is designed to turn very slowly, making a full revolution once a year. Next, slightly smaller, comes a pyramid, holding the executive of Comintern and turning once a month. Above this is a cylinder, housing the press office and revolving once a day.

At the very top is a hemisphere containing a radio station and making a complete turn every hour.

Tatlin believed that the perfect geometrical forms of the cube, pyramid, cylinder and hemisphere had an inherent beauty – and the fact that the tower was functional as well as being a monument added to its beauty. It was part of his revolutionary philosophy that beauty and usefulness complemented one another. An important feature of the geometrical structures is that they are visible through the framework and are faced largely in glass. People looking in from outside could see how the organization was functioning, in marked contrast to the hidden machinations of the Tsarist regime. The tower is a symbol of transparency.

Together with a group of students, Tatlin built a large wooden model of the tower in 1920. This was followed by others – some in wood, some in metal – which were exhibited and even carried around the streets in processions to show the people what the latest form of architectural propaganda was going to look like. A model was also displayed as an adjunct to a famous agitprop spectacular, *The Storming of the Winter Palace*, which was put on in Petrograd (St Petersburg) in 1920 to commemorate the revolution.

The tower did not get past the model stage. Tatlin seems not to have specified the exact details of the structure (the models varied somewhat in their details) and the enormous amounts of steel required would have been hard to come by in post-revolutionary Russia, which suffered an economic slump. The government had other priorities, such as putting food on people's plates. However, the influence of the tower lived on. Many artists saw the models, and the tower's thrusting, spiralling structure became one of the most famous works of the Constructivist movement in art.

None of the contemporary models survived, and for decades after Tatlin conceived it knowledge of the monument relied on a few faded photographs and drawings. But even in these faint images, the tower is easy to respond to – there is something about helical and spiral forms that is instantly attractive and their wide appeal reflects the collective spirit behind the idea. 'Invention', says Tatlin, is 'always the working out of impulses and desires of the collective, not of the individual.' Born out of a collective struggle, the design of the Monument to the Third International – in reproductions, on paper and as an idea – still provokes widespread admiration.

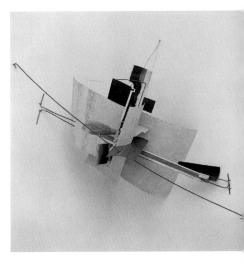

Complex Corner Relief *(1915) is one of Tatlin's abstract sculptures. It is designed to be attached to the walls in the corner of a room, so that it is poised, as if about to take flight.*

PLEASURE PAVILIONS

Erich Mendelsohn, 1920

Architecture as Sculpture

The architect Erich Mendelsohn was a pioneer Modernist. He was born in Allenstein, east Prussia (now Olszstyn, Poland) to Jewish parents. After training in Berlin and Munich, he began his architectural practice in Munich in 1918, and was soon successful. His Modernist designs for houses and factories showed a flair for handling materials such as steel and glass, and a very individual sense of form. Modernist buildings often looked like very plain rectilinear boxes of concrete or glass, but Mendelsohn's had a strong sense of form and shape, sometimes curving at the corners, sometimes with prominent, horizontal lines running across the building. From early in his career, he had a sculptor's touch.

Mendelsohn's most famous building is his most sculptural. This is the Einstein Tower, housing laboratories and an observatory, at Potsdam. The structure looks as if it has been moulded out of pale concrete. A low, spreading base, all curves and sloping walls, supports a four-floor tower topped by a dome-shaped observatory. The tower's walls curve – concave on one face, convex on another – and there is hardly a straight line to be seen. The tower's style is sometimes called Expressionist. When Einstein himself saw it, he looked at it for a long time in silence, then summed it up in one word: 'Organic'.

Mendelsohn never had the chance to complete such a sculptural building again. In the 1930s, he was forced to leave Germany, and he settled first in Britain then in the USA. He designed some fine buildings in these places but never anything as organic or Expressionist as the Einstein Tower. However, the notebooks he kept as a young man are full of drawings for sculptural concrete buildings, curving and twisting forms even more daring than the tower.

Some of these drawings are for skyscrapers; some for industrial buildings. One is a sketch called 'project for a hall' that looks like an early version of Sydney Opera House, fifty years before Jørn Utzon conceived it. A number of drawings are for unidentified structures inspired by the changing shapes of sand dunes that the architect observed on a visit to the

Mendelsohn did a number of rapid drawings when working out ideas for the Luckenwalde garden pavilion. This is one of the most organic – its curving forms radiating like parts of a shell.

Prussian coast. Another set are
apparently inspired by pieces
of music and have captions
such as 'Toccata in D major'
– these drawings feature
repeated lines and curves
that seem to be linked to
recurring phrases or rhythms
in music: Erich Mendelsohn
referred to architecture as
'formed rhythm'.

*This sketch for the pavilion
has an upright central section.
The series of indentations may
represent windows wrapping
around the building, producing
an effect similar to Mendelsohn's
Einstein Tower.*

A lot of the drawings fall
into the category of 'fantasy
architecture'. They were not meant to be built, but to act as
ideas for more practical buildings. But a few come directly
from one of Mendelsohn's commissions. The architect's
family were friendly with the Herrmanns, who were hat
manufacturers in Luckenwalde, in the state of Brandenberg,
eastern Germany. In 1919, Gustav Herrmann asked
Mendelsohn to design a small pavilion or summerhouse for
his garden at Luckenwalde (a few years later, he also designed
a new hat factory for the family). For the garden pavilion, the
architect eventually produced an octagonal wooden structure.

However, before he came up with the finished design,
Mendelsohn produced a series of much more interesting drafts,
in ever more sculptural form. These drawings, known as either
Pleasure Pavilions or Garden Pavilions, showed the way he
was thinking. Some of the forms curve in repeated patterns
like shells; some have ridged, domed roofs like spinning tops;
others have organic forms like the Einstein Tower. They all
look more like sculptures than buildings, and would really
have been possible only in a plastic material such as concrete.

Mendelsohn was baffled by the source of his 'inclination
towards the fantastic'. Scholars have suggested that it might
lie in the decorative style of the beginning of the twentieth
century: Art Nouveau. This style drew on a vocabulary of
curves, on sinuous lines and organic forms. The curvaceous
forms of Paris Métro stations or the work of people such as
Belgian designer Henri van de Velde are possible sources of
inspiration. The pavilions also have a passing resemblance to
the sculptural and curvaceous buildings of another great turn-
of-the-century architect, the Catalan Antoni Gaudí (see Hotel
Attraction entry on page 118).

Mendelsohn understood that what he was exploring was something far from ordinary, and puzzled about what it was that made him design structures such as this. He writes: 'With me the everyday becomes something more than the everyday. I do not really know if it is because of my inclination towards the fantastic.' But Mendelsohn goes on to say that his thinking is still firmly rooted in reality and the challenges of actually constructing buildings: 'Problems of symmetry, and of the elasticity of the building components, and of the closed contour and of methods of construction concern me at every line and act as discipline, self-criticism and a universal rule.'

Another of the architect's sketches combines one set of curves that embrace the building from front to back and another set that sweep up from the base.

While making the drawings for the Pleasure Pavilions, Mendelsohn was also hard at work on the Einstein Tower – building at Potsdam started in 1921. He was constantly puzzling away at how to build this organic, Expressionist, little building in the materials available, becoming confident that steel and concrete would answer the challenge and allow a new kind of structure:

Steel in combination with concrete, reinforced concrete, is the building material for formal expression, for the new style... the relation between support and load, this apparently eternal law, will also have to alter its image, for things support themselves which formerly had to be supported... Towers mount and grow out of themselves with their own power and spirit and soul.

But using these materials was not always easy. The architect had to modify the structure of the Einstein Tower during construction because the steel and concrete would not support the shape he originally planned – only then could the tower 'grow out of itself' in the way he wanted. Perhaps, these difficulties were the reason why the inventive and Expressionist Pleasure Pavilions, striking and unique as they were, never got built. As time went on, Mendelsohn's practice became busy with such practical and large-scale buildings as department stores, factories and houses. Thus, the architect had to devote his time to fresh challenges, and his adventurous designs for Gustav Herrmann stayed in his sketchbook.

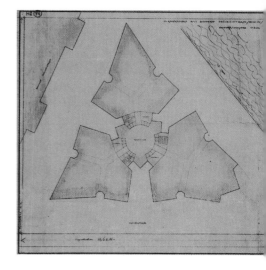

The floor plan shows not only the way in which the building uses the entire site but also how its shape (in effect three linked sections) enables natural light to find its way into the structure, with no desk too far away from an outside wall.

BERLIN, GERMANY

FRIEDRICHSTRASSE SKYSCRAPER

Ludwig Mies van der Rohe, 1922

A Crystalline Skyscraper Clad in Glass

In 1922, a design for a radically new kind of skyscraper appeared in Germany. The Friedrichstrasse Tower, by German architect Ludwig Mies van der Rohe, was not square, nor rectangular, nor even round. It was a unique crystalline shape and it was clad entirely in shining glass. On its proposed site in Berlin, next to traditional, low-rise buildings ornamented in the Classical style, it would have created a sensation. But it was too forward-looking and was never built. However, Mies's outstanding design has haunted and influenced architects of tall buildings ever since.

Its story began in 1921, when a new company, the Turmhaus Aktiengesellschaft (Tower House Company) announced a competition for designs for a new office building in Berlin. The site was a triangular plot next to the Friedrichstrasse railway station, and the competition asked for a 263ft- (80m-) tall building, accompanied by a properly calculated list of the usable floor space. There was a sizeable prize on offer, and the competition was attractive to architects in other ways, too: it was a high-profile site and large building projects were scarce.

From the point of view of Mies, the competition was a major opportunity. Before the First World War, he had been designing mostly small buildings – villas for middle-class clients – in the Classical style. However, he had become one of the many architects who thought that, after the disaster of the war, architecture should make a new start, going back to basics and not relying on the revivals of historical styles that had dominated architecture in the nineteenth century.

The 144 architects who entered the Turmhaus Aktiengesellschaft competition found various solutions to the challenging triangular site: the entries included round, triangular and star-shaped plans, many of them traditionally decorated in historical styles. None of them made use of the whole site, and with good reason: filling up the whole plot would mean that natural light could not reach the middle of the building. Architects had a rule of thumb that dictated that no one sitting in an office should be more than 25ft (7.5m) from a window.

Mies worked out a way of letting more light into the building while also making use of the entire site, to maximize the floor area. He did this with a unique plan consisting of three wedge-like shapes, linked at the centre of the plan but divided by light wells at the edges. As well as being an ingenious way of letting in more natural light, this was also one of the features that gave the tower its distinctive, crystalline form. No other building had such sharply pointed corners, or

The stark contrast between the shimmering form of Mies's glass skyscraper and the surrounding nineteenth-century Berlin architecture is made clear in this montage of photograph and architect's drawing.

presented such a dramatic combination of planes and spaces to its street facade.

However, the thing that really set Mies's skyscraper apart was the fact that it has no conventional walls. Its steel framework is clad entirely, from top to bottom, in glass. No one had ever designed a building like this before. The skyscrapers of Chicago and New York, which inspired the German architects who entered the Berlin competition, had steel frames hidden by a cladding of masonry. Some had large windows, but these were always set in a substantial surrounding framework. They also had features such as stone plinths at pavement level, grand doorways set in decorative stone frames, and ornament in a historical style such as Classical or Gothic. Mies did away with all of this at a stroke.

Mies probably got the idea of this crystalline glass cladding from looking at photographs of skyscrapers under construction. He clearly admired the appearance of their steel frames, as well as their engineering. Mies contrasted the character of the framework with the sham decoration of the masonry of conventional skyscrapers: 'Only in the course of their construction do skyscrapers show their bold, structural character, and then the impression made by their soaring skeletal frames is overwhelming. On the other hand, when the facades are later covered with masonry this impression is destroyed…' What was left when a skyscraper's structure was hidden away behind meaningless decoration was, according to Mies, 'a senseless and trivial chaos of forms'.

The architect could also justify his design in terms of functionalism – the architectural doctrine that a building's form should be determined by the needs of its users. From a functionalist point of view, the glass walls and crystalline shape were justified by the need to get lots of natural light into the

The architect's variant design has curved walls and is taller than the Friedrichstrasse original, but uses the same glass 'skin' and the same interplay of indentations and protrusions.

building, while keeping the floor space as large as possible. The design certainly succeeded in these terms. Even allowing for the fact that Mies's building has an unusually large floor-to-ceiling height (to let in yet more light, while reducing the possible number of storeys), he crammed more square footage onto the site than his competitors. Revolutionary in form, stunning to look at and functionally sound, the tower should have been a triumph.

But Mies did not win the competition. His design was too unusual to win, and was dismissed by the judges, along with other impressive contenders such as strong, unornamented, modern-looking proposals by Hugo Häring and Hans Poelzig. The panel favoured instead a squat, fifteen-storey building clad in brick, which was not built either. The site had to wait decades for a full redevelopment, with a curvaceous structure designed by Marc Braun, in 1992.

Neither the judges nor most commentators picked out Mies's design for special praise or comment, but the architect did not let the glass skyscraper idea go. He published both the Friedrichstrasse design and a variation on the same theme in the magazine *Frühlicht* in 1922. The variant design is taller than the Friedrichstrasse Tower and has curved walls, but with a similar plan, using indentations and protrusions to allow natural light into every part of each floor. This design was not intended for a specific client – it was Mies's way of developing his idea in the hope that at some point a suitable site and client would come along.

The *Frühlicht* article together with Mies's surviving drawings helped keep the design alive in people's minds. The drawings are dramatic and impressive, especially a gigantic one (68 × 48in/173 × 122cm) that was so big that, when the architect left Nazi Germany to move to the USA, in 1938, he was unable to take it with him. In the post-war period, the drawing began to be widely published in architectural books and magazines, and, in 1964, Mies was able to get it back from East Germany. It was exhibited at New York's Museum of Modern Art and has been widely published and exhibited since then, becoming a favourite image for architects to study. By this time, the idea of a glass-clad skyscraper was no longer so revolutionary. In the 1950s and 1960s, it had become normal for tall buildings to have large expanses of glass and thin 'curtain walls'. Mies's Friedrichstrasse Tower is accepted as their most important ancestor.

TRIBUNE TOWER BY ELIEL SAARINEN

Eliel Saarinen, 1922

A Visionary Modernist Building that Set the Style for Later Skyscrapers

On 10 June 1922, the *Chicago Tribune* announced one of the most enticing architectural competitions of the early twentieth century: '$100,000 in prizes to architects. Seventy-five years old today, the *Tribune* seeks surpassing beauty in new home on Michigan Boulevard.' The prize was a huge attraction: often the winner of an architectural prize got simply the kudos of victory and the percentage fee the architect usually earned on the designs.

The proposed building was high profile, and the *Tribune* was asking for something special – a building to reflect the success and prestige of Chicago and its newspaper:

- 'to adorn with a monument of enduring beauty this city, in which the *Tribune* has prospered so amazingly;

- 'to create a structure which will be an inspiration and a model for generations of newspaper publishers;

- 'to provide a new and beautiful home worthy of the world's greatest newspaper.'

So there was a demand for beauty, a monument, a stand-out building – a far cry from the usual commercial request for the maximum amount of office space on the smallest possible budget.

The location was significant. Chicago was a major industrial centre and a city of vast importance. It had been the birthplace of the skyscraper after a fire had destroyed about 3.3 sq. miles (8.5 sq. km) of the city centre in 1871 and developers started to build tall to take full advantage of the limited land in the downtown area. The opportunity to design a tall office building in Chicago was, therefore, the chance to make a major architectural statement in the 'home' of the skyscraper.

So the *Tribune*'s announcement was a call many architects found impossible to resist. Even the second- and third-place buildings commanded substantial prizes and would get plenty of publicity. Entries began to pour in from the major cities of the USA, and then from abroad. By the time the judges got

OPPOSITE *Saarinen's design looks familiar today because many later American skyscrapers use similar setbacks and the same vertical lines sweeping up the facades.*

to work, there were some 260 designs to choose from. They varied a lot, given the restrictions of site and the stipulation that the building should be not more than 394ft (120m) tall. There were Gothic skyscrapers, Classical ones, pared-down Modernist ones. There were Adolf Loos's skyscraper in the form of an ancient Greek column (see Tribune Tower by Adolf Loos entry on page 146) and Walter Gropius and Adolf Meyer's steel and glass structure that looked more like a cluster of buildings than a single structure. There were towers that came to a point and flat-topped towers.

In the end, the judges chose one of the Gothic entries: the design from New York architects John Mead Howells and Raymond M. Hood, which is topped with an octagonal 'lantern' feature ringed with flying buttresses. It is certainly a strong design giving the *Tribune* more than its share of beauty and monumentality and creating a landmark for Chicago. The clients were pleased.

Many architects, however, preferred another design – the one that came second. This was by Finnish designer Eliel Saarinen. Saarinen was nearly fifty years old and a moderately successful architect and town planner in Finland, but was not well known in the USA. His design is much more modern-looking than the winner – it also takes a cue from the upward emphasis of Gothic architecture but without covering the building in medieval ornament. As Saarinen himself said, the design is all about verticality. Perpendicular lines (actually the masonry between ranks of windows) sweep up the sides of the building, leading the eye upwards until the point just over halfway up where the tower begins to narrow in a series of four setbacks. But the verticals still continue, leading the viewer's gaze right to the very top.

The design is highly effective visually, and the setbacks became a key principle of skyscraper building – that a tall tower should get narrower towards the top, letting in more light to the streets at its base and reducing the tendency of streets lined with tall buildings to become unfriendly 'canyons'. Saarinen did not invent the setback – the idea was beginning to be adopted, anyway. But his use of it caught the eye of people in the profession. Hundreds of architects were watching the competition eagerly to see who would win. One of these was Louis Sullivan, the greatest of the previous generation of Chicago architects, a highly influential figure and mentor to others such as Frank Lloyd Wright. Sullivan praised the

Saarinen design and said that it showed the way forward for future tall buildings. So the Saarinen design received the approval of the older generation. As it happens, it appealed to the young, too. Its shape was also well suited to the Art Deco style, which came to dominate architecture in the late 1920s and 1930s. It seemed to fit with the times.

Even though it did not win, Saarinen's design was an architectural triumph. It attracted imitators as soon as the competition was over, and many later architects copied its two main features – the vertical lines and the setbacks. Even Raymond Hood, architect of the winning Gothic design, was influenced, in his designs for New York's Rockefeller Centre. The tower's closest imitators were the architects of Houston's Gulf Building of 1929 (now the J. P. Morgan Chase Building), which follows the profile of Saarinen's design closely.

Architects found the notion of the setback hugely adaptable. You could vary it in many ways, and the resulting changes in profile, which introduce more corners into the building, can give a tall tower increased visual interest. Saarinen himself was pleased with his colleagues' response to the design. He was living in Finland and had little work. He had never designed a skyscraper before. Now his work was attracting attention in North America, bringing him the prospect of more work there. He moved to the USA shortly afterwards.

Saarinen became an influential figure when he settled in the USA. He designed the campus of the Cranbrook Educational Community, Michigan, and became head of the Cranbrook Academy of Art. Cranbrook, intended to be the American equivalent of the German Bauhaus, was soon an important school of art and design – among Saarinen's pupils were talented individuals such as Charles and Ray Eames, who became prominent Modernist designers.

Presumably, Saarinen did not win the competition because his tower wasn't enough of a 'monument' to convince the judges fully. The gesture of the Gothic lantern in the winning design was more like what they wanted. But Saarinen had posterity on his side. Many architects and critics think his was the best design, and, above all, he received his much-valued accolade from Louis Sullivan. The older architect, too, saw that history would come down in Saarinen's favour. The following year, Sullivan wrote a paean of praise to the Finn's unbuilt tower. It is not, he writes, 'a lonely cry in the wilderness, it is a voice, resonant and rich, ringing amid the wealth and joy of life.'

The winning design with its Gothic lantern featured on countless postcards and documentary photographs of the city, and became a familiar part of the Chicago scene.

TRIBUNE TOWER BY ADOLF LOOS

Adolf Loos, 1922

A Tower in the Form of a Classical Column

Among the 260 architects who entered the competition to design the *Chicago Tribune* tower in 1922 were a number from outside the USA. Altogether, architects from twenty-three countries sent in designs. Some of them were ultra-modern plans, others drew heavily on the architecture of the past, such as the winner, the Gothic tower designed by John Mead Howells and Raymond M. Hood. The winner took medieval architecture for its inspiration, but others used even older sources, drawing on the Classical architecture of ancient Greece and Rome. Perhaps, the most surprising of all the designs was by one of the European entrants – Czech-born and Vienna-based Adolf Loos. His drawings show a skyscraper in the form of an enormous Classical column, square for the eleven floors of its pedestal and base, circular for the rest of its height, with a simple, square, slab-like top. The circular part of the building is clad in gleaming, black granite while the lower part is of brick and terracotta.

This design is surprising today because we are used to thinking of tall buildings as quintessentially modern and as structures that take advantage of the latest in technology and design to get them to the heights they need to be. Modern office buildings are not usually in an antique style. To be sure, some of the early skyscrapers of Chicago and New York are in the Gothic style, and others are richly decorated, though often in a twentieth-century style – some of the most famous, such as the Empire State and Chrysler Buildings in New York, are pure Art Deco. A Doric column seems to come from another world.

The surprise was even greater because of the source of the design. Loos was a famous Modernist. In 1910, he had given a lecture (later published as an essay) called 'Ornament and crime', in which he had rejected the old ways of design, decrying all kinds of architectural ornament as criminal. Ornament, said Loos, derives from the same sensibility as the work of the graffiti artist or the criminal with a tattooed chest. Loos preferred buildings that did not take their cue from outward appearance but were driven by the users' needs.

The perspective drawing by Loos, with its low viewpoint and strong contrast between the black granite cladding and pale sky, emphasizes the monumentality of the design.

He seemed to be the last person in the world to be reaching into the history books for the design of a skyscraper.

The Chicago column was not quite as surprising to contemporaries, however. They did not see an absolute break between ancient and modern architecture. People even compared skyscrapers to columns, likening the main body of the building to the column's main portion or shaft, the entrance level, treated slightly differently visually, to the column's base, and the cornice at the top to its capital. This metaphor was coined by the American architect Louis Sullivan, a noted influence on Loos – the European architect was almost certainly aware of Sullivan's notion.

But Sullivan was not advocating building a tower in the precise form of a column – he was just making a comparison and pointing out how architects might make use of the similarities in the details of a design. Several of the entrants of the Chicago competition, though, did take the idea to its logical conclusion. A number of them produced designs with a column-like element, although none of these was as uncompromising as the one by Loos, and his rivals were crude by comparison.

Loos had a slightly different take and another rationale. He took his cue, like any good competition entrant, from the brief. The *Tribune* wanted the most beautiful office building in the world, and one that would act as a monument for the city of Chicago. The notion of a monument set Loos thinking. If a structure was to have a monumental form it would need different treatment from, say, a house, which could have a plain facade, with features such as windows placed where they were needed, or a regular office block, which could have a simple, flat facade, with regular fenestration. A monument, by contrast, should be striking, memorable, lasting and distinctive.

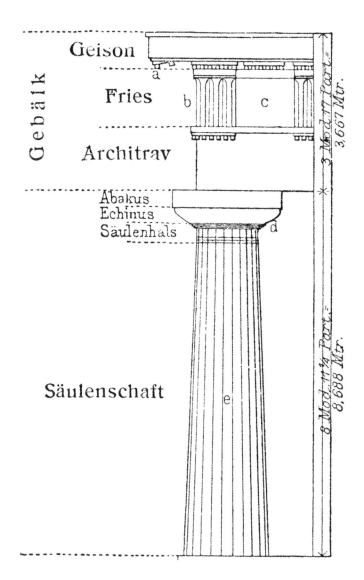

This diagram from a German architectural textbook shows an ancient Greek Doric column – the kind that inspired Loos when he designed his competition entry. Loos imitated both the fluted body of the column and the square stone (the abacus) that is placed at the top.

How should an architect go about creating a memorable, lasting monument for Chicago? In a report he wrote to accompany the design, Loos considered the possibilities. One way would be to make the building taller than any other – but someone could come along and build still taller, and in any case the *Tribune* had ruled this out by imposing a height restriction: they wanted the tower to be 394ft (120m) tall or less. Another possibility would be to invent a new style, to create something that was newer-looking than anything else in the neighbourhood. But the new soon turns into the old – as Loos puts it: 'the fashion in forms changes very quickly, just like that of clothing'. Such a building would not be distinctive for long.

Drawing on tradition and harking back to monumental structures such as Trajan's Column in Rome seemed to Loos a better idea. So he took one of the most simple Classical column types – the Doric – and enlarged it into an office tower. The floors in the main part of the building are round, with a central lift shaft giving access to a series of wedge-shaped or trapezoidal rooms. It seemed to work, giving the newspaper the memorable building it wanted, while also accommodating the required office space. At the top of the tower, instead of the statue that many monumental columns bear, is a simple plain abacus – the tower itself is the monument, and some critics have seen the lack of a statue as a way of saying that its occupant – the newspaper – was a true pillar of the community. The structure's round form and shiny cladding also made it unusual enough – some would say unsubtle and bizarre enough – to stand out in Chicago, a city already bristling with tall buildings.

The judges did not share Loos's logic, and his design did not even gain second or third place after the winning Gothic tower by Hood and Howells. It is not known whether they were put off by the outward appearance of the building, or by the odd-shaped rooms inside. Loos probably knew he was an outsider with little chance in this big architectural race. But the final part of his report shows his confidence in his design, and his pre-emptive defiance: 'The big Greek column will be built, if not for the *Chicago Tribune* then elsewhere, if not by me then by some other architect.' Loos never got another chance to build his tower, or to design on such a large scale. In his last years, he worked mainly on houses for middle-class clients in central Europe, buildings that are still admired – for their artful planning and their modernity, not for any references to the ancient world.

CHAPTER 5
RADIANT CITIES

In the late 1920s and 1930s, architects increasingly explored Modernist design.

This could mean many different things: functionalism, a lack of ornament, or flat-roofed buildings with white walls. Above all, modernist architects used materials such as steel and glass to redesign not just individual buildings but also entire cities. Following the lead of Mies van der Rohe's glass-clad Berlin tower (see Friedrichstrasse Skyscraper entry on page 138), they used more and more glass, so that buildings became almost transparent, and the views out of them were broader than ever before.

Glass does not have the insulating qualities of a conventional masonry wall, but widespread mains electricity allowed architects not only to heat and air-condition interiors with ease, but also to light both buildings and city streets brightly. The glow of electric light was one thing that led Le Corbusier to name his most famous city plan Ville Radieuse (Radiant City). Architects also explored the sculptural qualities of glass – one result being the bizarre, flowing shapes of Hermann Finsterlin's designs for glass houses.

Finsterlin's plans for curious tubular glass structures might have proved impossible to realize, but many buildings of this period were highly practical and functional. Architects as

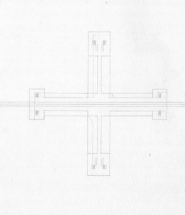

the potential of

COUPE

different as the Modernist Walter Gropius and the pioneer of streamlining Norman Bel Geddes analysed how a building might be used and tried to develop forms that would give its occupants what they needed. Functional thinking like this lay behind both Gropius's Total Theatre and Bel Geddes's Aerial Restaurant for the Chicago exhibition. Both might well have been built if other people involved in these projects had been more supportive of their architects.

However, many of these designs, though justifiable functionally, proved impractical in terms of structure or, especially, cost. Two of the most revolutionary – the 'horizontal skyscrapers' or Cloud Irons devised for Moscow by the artist El Lissitzky and the Apartments on Bridges proposed around Manhattan in New York City by the illustrator Hugh Ferriss – failed to get off the drawing board mainly for these reasons. Cost also stymied more traditional buildings such as the grand plan of Edwin Lutyens for a Byzantine-style Catholic cathedral for Liverpool. It is part of the architect's job to produce plans that work in terms of money as well as function. But it would still be wrong to dismiss the work of Lissitzky, Ferriss and Lutyens. Their bold designs, in the form of models, plans or atmospheric drawings, still provide ideas for other designers, and offer the rest of us something to marvel at.

SOUS-SOL

SOL

0   200

CLOUD IRONS

El Lissitzky, 1923–5

Horizontal Skyscrapers, Propped High Above Moscow

The idea of horizontal skyscrapers seems to be a contradiction in terms, but one Russian designer tried to make it real. Arguing that humans are happier in horizontal than in vertical environments, he developed some of the most remarkable structures ever conceived to address the challenges of urban growth. Few architects would have even thought of designing buildings such as these – but the creator of the horizontal skyscrapers or Cloud Irons was not an architect at all.

Lazar Markovich Lissitzky, known as El Lissitzky, was one of the most versatile artists of the Russian revolutionary period. Born in 1890 in Pochinok near Smolensk, Lissitzky first drew on his Jewish heritage as an illustrator of Yiddish children's books, but became famous as an abstract artist and graphic designer. He and his friend Kazimir Malevich were pioneers of the art movement known as Suprematism, in which abstract paintings were created using simple geometrical shapes (circles, squares and lines, for example) in a narrow range of colours. The results could have enormous impact, but were very often flat and two-dimensional in effect. Lissitzky took the style in a new direction, producing more layered compositions and, therefore, a greater feeling of three-dimensional space, in works he called Prouns (a term said to come from a Russian phrase meaning 'project for the renewal of art', though there are other possible derivations). These paintings have an architectural quality, and some of the shapes in them seem to suggest walls, floors and even whole buildings. All these Suprematist works, so radically different from any previous art, became closely linked with the seismic political changes brought about by the Russian revolution of 1917.

Lissitzky was fascinated with architecture, and with using art to solve problems that Russia faced after the revolution. Russian cities needed to expand – there was a severe housing shortage and a pressing need for better public transport. Lissitzky was not convinced that the American way – building tall towers to house offices and apartments – was the right one. He thought that vertical buildings were unnatural. People

cannot fly; they are happier with horizontal movement than with travelling up and down; walking is easier than climbing. So, in 1925, he devised a way of constructing a horizontal building raised in the air, so that it did not use up valuable ground space already occupied by roads and low-rise buildings. The Cloud Iron was born.

Cloud Irons are slab-shaped buildings, each with a flat roof, three storeys and several horizontal wings, mounted on a trio of sturdy supports or pylons. The pylons raise the slabs 164ft (50m) into the air, and the slabs themselves span a total length of about 590ft (180m), overhanging the pylons dramatically

Although they are massive, the Cloud Irons were designed to be sited at road junctions, so they would overhang roads and tramlines rather than the nearby houses. Lissitzky sketched in the surrounding buildings as simple boxes, to demonstrate how his structures would fit onto the site.

Proun 1, a painting of 1914, shows how Lissitzky's art, although abstract, sometimes depicted geometrical structures that resembled boxes, buildings or walls.

so that they appear to float in the air. In a forward-looking step towards the integration of architecture and transport, one of the three pylons in each structure is designed to continue underground, where it becomes a subway station; the other pylons incorporate ground-level tram-stop shelters.

The horizontal skyscrapers are designed with a steel framework and in the drawings and photomontages that the artist made they have curtain walls of glass. The aim was for interiors that are both light and well ventilated, but also for buildings that, while structurally sound, do not look too solid. One of the fascinating things about the designs is how they matched very large, chunky forms with an almost transparent skin. This kind of construction was very new in 1925, but would become much more familiar in the decades to come in glass-clad skyscrapers by architects such as Ludwig Mies van der Rohe (see Freidrichstrasse Skyscraper entry on page 138).

The visual effect of the Cloud Irons was dramatic. In Lissitzky's drawings they seemed to hover over the cityscape like alien forms. The revolution had shown that Russia could withstand dramatic and violent change, and they seem to show architecture undergoing a revolution, too. The Suprematist style of the buildings, with its similarity to Lissitzky's paintings, made this point clear. The artist was suggesting that buildings in a style associated with the revolution would show people that the effects of political change could be felt in their very homes and workplaces: the revolution could benefit people in a tangible, practical way.

Suprematist buildings did not blend harmoniously with the more conventional architecture of Moscow, so Lissitzky worked hard to try to make the forms of the structures as balanced and elegant as he could, putting all the skill he had developed balancing shapes in his two-dimensional art to work in these three-dimensional structures. The forms were honed over a period of time. During much of the 1920s, he was working outside Russia, with extended periods in Germany, meeting many artistic movers and shakers at the Congress of Progressive Artists in Düsseldorf in 1922, working with Mies van der Rohe in Berlin, and collaborating with the cutting-edge artists and designers at the Bauhaus in Weimar. As well as speaking Russian and Yiddish, the language of his Jewish family, Lissitzky was fluent in German, so it is natural that many of his drawings give the Cloud Irons their German name, Wolkenbügel. However, Lissitzky's principal collaborator on the buildings was a Dutch designer and architect, Mart Stam, who was also part of the Bauhaus circle. Stam was another versatile figure, who devised chairs made of tubular metal (a concept later taken up by Bauhaus designer Marcel Breuer) as well as buildings.

Lissitzky was particularly concerned about siting the structures carefully. He proposed eight Cloud Irons, each positioned at a major intersection on the ring road around central Moscow. Each building pointed towards the Kremlin in the centre of the city. As they were to be identically designed, he suggested painting them in different colours so that they could be distinguished easily. Sadly, he left only monochrome drawings of the structures, so we have to imagine the full impact of these colourful buildings looming over Moscow's skyline like Suprematist paintings made three-dimensional.

As a teacher and book illustrator, Lissitzky knew that it was important to communicate and publicize his ideas, so he wrote several articles about his creations – one in *ASNOVA News* (the journal of Russia's Association of New Architects) and another in the German art publication *Das Kunstblatt*. Articles such as these ensured that the Cloud Irons, unbuilt mainly because of a shortage of materials, remained well known to architects and others interested in design. Their striking forms and their very pared-down, functional-looking appearance fascinated architects, increasingly so as the profession became more and more engaged with Modernist design. Lissitzky's stunning drawings and photomontages, created by a graphic artist of the first rank, have ensured that his buildings have become among the best-known examples of phantom architecture.

GLASS HOUSE

Hermann Finsterlin, 1924

*Expressionist Architecture Sculpted out of
Transparent Materials*

Hermann Finsterlin had the oddest career of any architect. He
began studying science in Munich. Then, on a moonlit night
on top of a mountain in Bavaria, he is said to have realized that
he should be an artist, so switched to painting and philosophy.
He became an associate of a number of German Expressionist
painters and of two great architects: the pioneer Modernist
Walter Gropius and the Modernist and Expressionist Erich
Mendelsohn, who became a lifelong friend.

Finsterlin worked with Gropius on an exhibition of work by
unknown architects in 1919, after which he developed a series
of unrealized architectural projects. When the Nazis came to
power in the 1930s, he was commissioned to produce portraits
of prominent citizens and wall paintings for official buildings
– a job he attempted to avoid but was eventually forced to
do under the threat of imprisonment. A lot of his work was
destroyed in bombing during the Second World War, and
although he survived to the 1980s no building that he designed
was ever constructed. However, the extraordinary contorted
and sculptural shapes of his architectural drawings linger in
the memory and have had a lasting architectural influence.

With his background in natural science, Finsterlin was
fascinated by the structures of animal bodies. He marvelled at
the skeletons and skins of creatures such as craneflies, water
boatmen, frogs, toads and tortoises, comparing their bodies
to structures with vaults and columns. He asks: 'What barrel
vault, however modern, can be compared with the parabola of
a mammalian thorax, what column can be compared with the
silhouetted lines of the noble limbs of animals?' He wanted to
transfer this sense of structural wonder to his own buildings,
imagining interiors that would be like being inside some sort of
vast gland, habitable digestive tract or giant womb.

This use of natural forms underlies structures such as
Finsterlin's Glass House. In his drawing of the Glass House,
forms twist this way and that, curling around one another like
so much visceral tubing. They pile up with abandon or stretch

*OPPOSITE Finsterlin produced
many drawings of buildings made
up of curvaceous, often organic,
shapes. Their concrete outer walls
are frequently brightly coloured.*

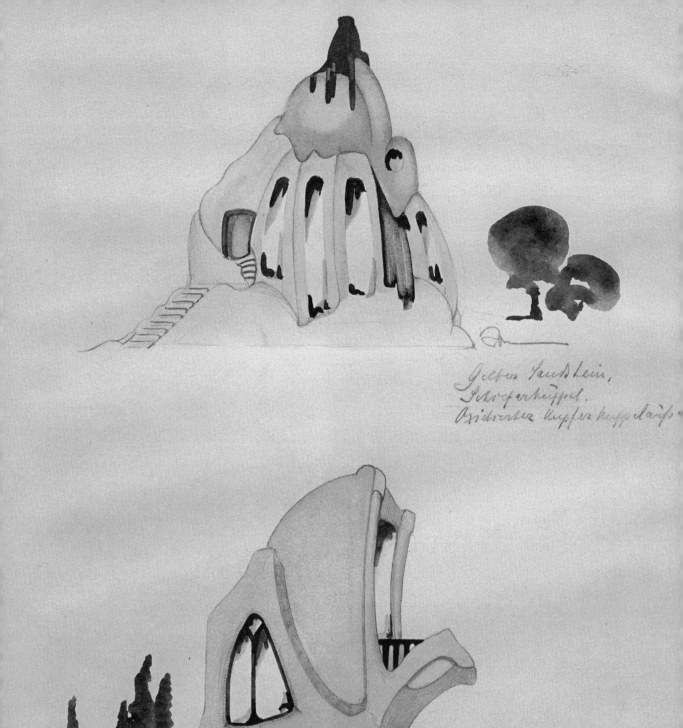

Gelber Sandstein.
Schieferkuppel.
Oxidiertes Kupfer Kuppeldach

Getönter Beton.
Beton-brahmen, galerie

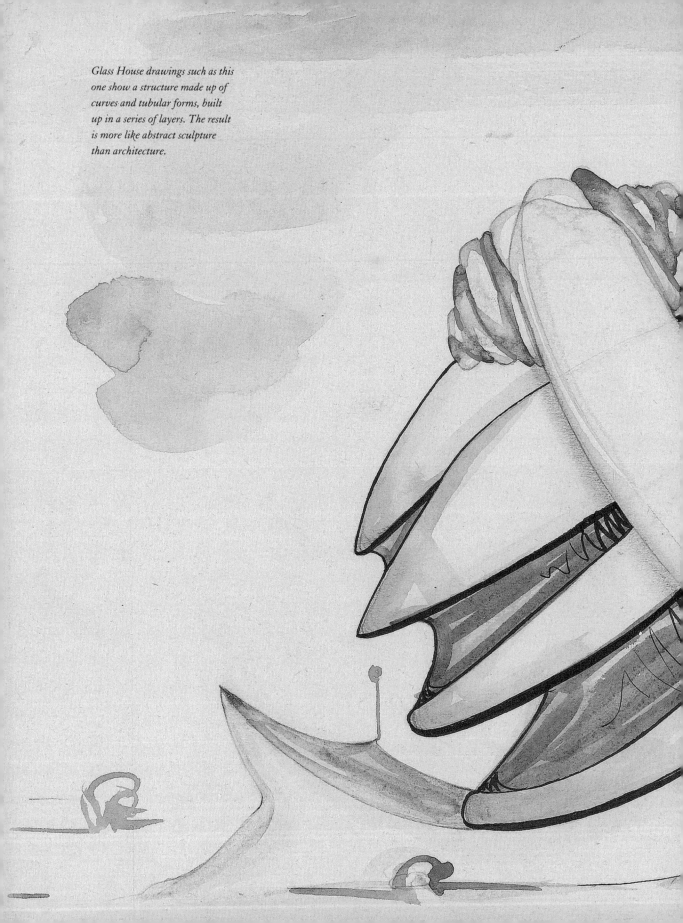

Glass House drawings such as this one show a structure made up of curves and tubular forms, built up in a series of layers. The result is more like abstract sculpture than architecture.

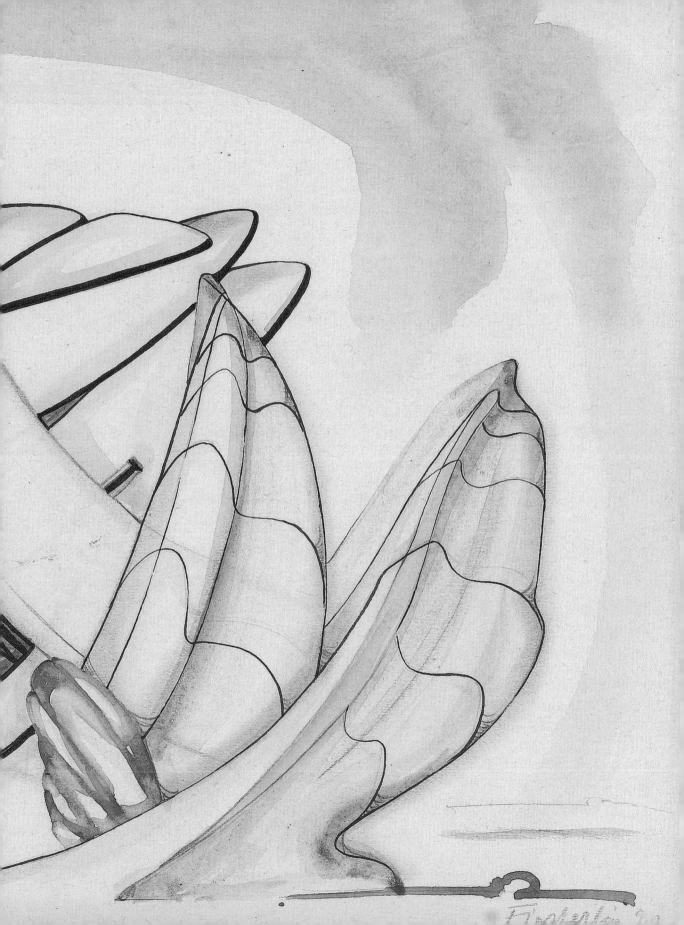

towards the sky without visible means of support. Harder-edged elements stick out like enormous dinosaur bones. The conventional language of architecture – walls, windows, roofs, storeys, facades – seems to have little to do with these structures. Their language is more sculptural and they appear indebted as much to Surrealism as to Expressionism. They seem, quite literally, to be out of this world.

What was Finsterlin doing drawing these apparently impractical buildings? He seems to have done many of his designs quickly, and the marks he made have been compared to the 'automatic writing' that some spiritualists claim to be done under the influence of the supernatural. Some of the drawings have a dream-like quality, and one is labelled 'Traum auf Glas' (Dream in glass). Many of the buildings look unbuildable, or buildable only in a world in which humans have managed to apply the principles of biological structure to architectural construction.

Part of what Finsterlin was up to was trying to make a new start. He and some of his fellow architects were dismayed by the poor design of many Modernist houses and apartments. First of all, they felt that modern architecture seemed dull. They were looking for something fresher, more imaginative, more adventurous; they did not just want technological advantages and the straight-lined, straight-laced 'machines for living in' promised by arch-Modernists such as Le Corbusier. Modernism was efficient, cutting-edge and based on the latest technology, but seemed to Finsterlin to lack soul or imagination. As one of his colleagues, Adolf Behne, puts it: 'All architecture is phantastic. And if the time clamours a hundred times for new patents, patents do not help much, without imagination. Speculators can build walls, we call for building.' Gropius, writing about his 'unknown architects' exhibition in 1919, made similar points: '… objects shaped by need and utility cannot fulfil the longing for a fundamentally new world of beauty'.

In taking this course, Finsterlin was rebelling against the rigidity of modern architecture. He did not want to be hemmed in by the relentless right angles of conventional building, especially of the Modernist building that was becoming increasingly fashionable. Finsterlin wanted to replace the straight lines of Modernism with something more fluid. In his writings he uses words such as flux, mutation, flowing and hybridization to describe the qualities in life that he thinks should be reflected in design. Finsterlin's buildings flow.

It was at around the same time that Erich Mendelsohn's drawings of equally flowing but more buildable structures (see Pleasure Pavilions entry on page 134) were exhibited, and that Mendelsohn, Finsterlin, Gropius and other architects began a sort of club-by-correspondence called the Glass Chain. Members of the Glass Chain sent each other a series of theoretical and sometimes mystical letters about architecture, writing under pseudonyms (Finsterlin was 'Prometh', after Prometheus, Greek god of creation and fire). The fanciful architecture of the Glass House fits well into this milieu.

This route away from Modernism towards fantasy is clearest when Finsterlin is drawing on his distinctive natural forms. This tendency, now known as biomorphism – is one of Finsterlin's enduring influences. Since the 1960s, with a range of buildings from the Pompidou Centre in Paris, with its exterior pipes and ducts (often called 'bowellist'), to the diaphanous structures of groups such as Coop Himmelb(l)au, Finsterlin's ideas have seemed increasingly relevant. Recent architecture's use of inflatable structures and tent-like forms continues this tendency.

Developments such as these are due partly to innovative architects seeking new forms, partly through the very advances in technology that Finsterlin and his friends sometimes said were irrelevant. Using the technology of the 1920s, Finsterlin's designs look impossible – even though some contemporaries said that it would be possible to build them using concrete, glass and steel. Today, with digital help in getting the curves right and technological advances in glass, plastics and the rest, they are more viable. But their true importance is in their ability to encourage architects and designers to explore the boundaries between building and the natural world.

VILLE RADIEUSE

Le Corbusier, 1924

High-Rise in a Green Setting: Le Corbusier's
Prototype for Modern Living

The Swiss-French architect Charles-Edouard Jeanneret, known as Le Corbusier, is one of the most influential of all twentieth-century architects. He is famous as the creator of outstanding houses that brought a new sense of space to domestic architecture, as the designer of large Unités d'habitation that offered a new form of high-density urban architecture, and as a city planner of daring and vision. He was many other things too – a painter, writer, designer of furniture and one of the creators of the style known as Brutalism.

Le Corbusier had a clear sense that architecture should respond to the needs and pressures of modern life. People who drive cars, are surrounded by modern gadgets and machinery, and live at the fast pace of the twentieth century had different architectural needs from the Victorians; the modern city, with its rapid growth and variety of functions, needs a different approach from cities such as Paris or London, which have evolved over centuries.

He also hated the unplanned nature of the traditional city, with its changing vistas, vastly varying buildings, streets that sometimes curve and are sometimes straight – everything due to the accidents of time. As the art critic Robert Hughes points out: 'being random was loathed by Le Corbusier'. So the architect sought to impose order everywhere. He created his own system of proportions, based on those of the human body. He developed a theory of house design founded on five basic principles. He designed a system of modular building construction, the Dom-Ino system, which consisted of standard-sized concrete slabs and uprights, which could be clad with a range of different walls and windows, and he began to propose new city designs, based on a more logical and more modern approach.

Le Corbusier felt that American cities, with their grid plans and skyscrapers, might be the best model for the modern city. Grid planning is logical and the Americans' use of high-rise allowed the high density needed as populations exploded and

OPPOSITE *Among Le Corbusier's many drawings for the Ville Radieuse are a number of plans. They show the way in which he used a rectilinear grid and arranged the city in a series of zones.*

OVERLEAF *The city's skyscrapers (Gratte-ciels) have a cross-shaped plan, with four slender arms allowing each room to have plenty of natural light. The site plan for a skyscraper shows how carefully the architect worked out the traffic flow on the access roads and surrounding highways.*

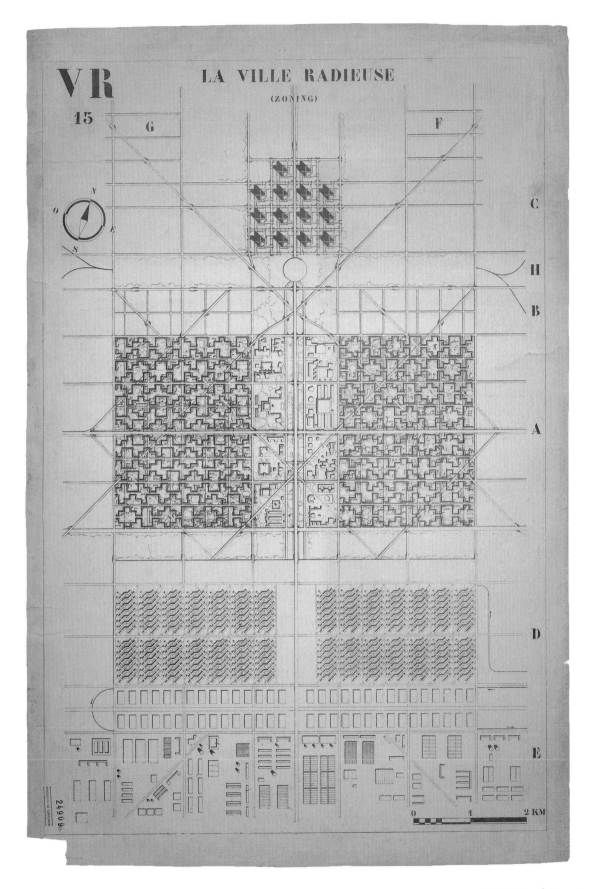

LA VILLE RADIEUSE

(ZONING)

VR

15

G

F

C

H

B

A

D

E

N
O
E
S

0   1   2 KM

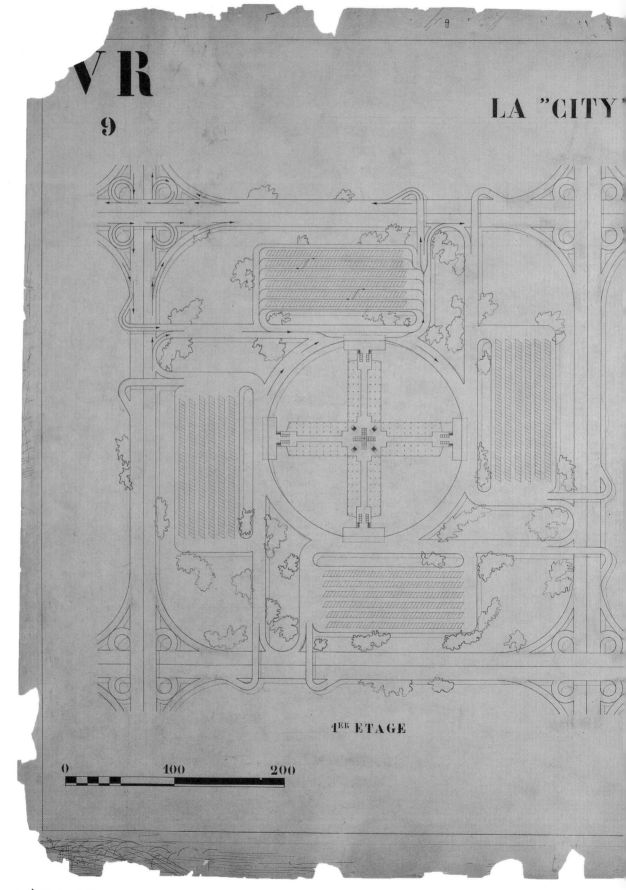

1ᴱᴿ ÉTAGE

0   100   200

LES GRATTE-CIELS

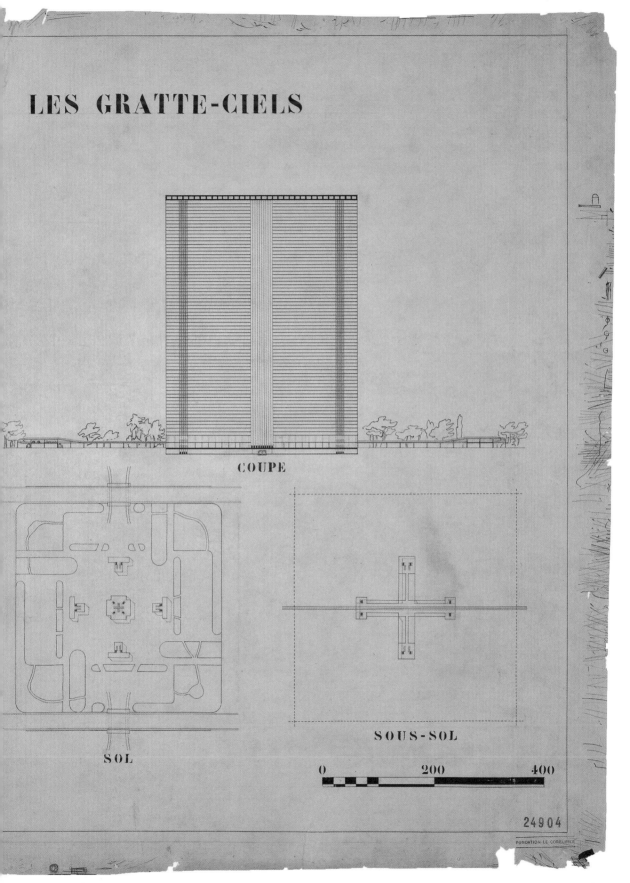

COUPE

SOL

SOUS-SOL

0   200   400

24904

FONDATION LE CORBUSIER

downtown prices soared. In an interview in 1932, he says: 'The United States is the adolescent of the contemporary world and New York is her expression of enthusiasm, juvenility, boldness, enterprise, pride and vanity. New York stands on the brink of the world like a hero…'

But even New York, with its exciting cityscape, skyscrapers and grid plan, has its limitations. For Le Corbusier, the skyscrapers were too close together, the streets too narrow, the buildings and green spaces not sufficiently integrated. Clearly, an ambitious planner would want to start again from scratch. So Le Corbusier began to create proposals for a new kind of town plan – an ideal city, not one designed for a specific location. He made several city plans along these lines, and by the 1920s was getting close to his ideal with a 'Ville contemporaine' (also known as the 'City for three million inhabitants'), a plan of 1922. Some of the key features were clusters of cross-planned skyscrapers set among parkland, lower-rise residential buildings, a central hub containing rail and bus stations, and the zoning of different types of buildings.

Le Corbusier's ideas about the city reached their mature and complete form in the Ville Radieuse (Radiant City) of 1924–30, which adopts most of these features. Ville Radieuse is fully zoned – different parts of the city are set aside for specific functions. A group of office towers about 656ft (200m) tall form the business district. Nearby is a transport hub linking this zone to the residential districts on either side. The residential buildings are in the form of mid-rise blocks some 164ft (50m) tall. These structures are not simply apartment blocks. They are the mixed-use structures that Le Corbusier called Unités d'habitation, which incorporate laundries, restaurants, shops, childcare and recreational facilities as well as apartments. They are set in parkland that provides places for the occupants to relax, play sports, socialize and so on. Well away from the office towers and residential zone is the city's industrial area. The overall plan is on a linear grid, and Le Corbusier's idea was that it could be expanded as needed and adapted to suit different settings.

A notable feature of the buildings – both the tall office towers and the lower residential blocks – is that they were raised above the ground on concrete pillars, or pilotis as Le Corbusier called them. This meant that the ground beneath them is clear, and helps to create the impression that these very large buildings do not so much occupy the land as hover

Le Corbusier preferred to place housing and related functions in mid-rise blocks, joined at right angles to create sheltered green spaces. These blocks were the ancestors of the architect's later Unités d'habitation.

above it. The parkland surrounding the apartments and offices hardly seemed to be interrupted by the buildings at all.

The zones are linked by roads on more than one level, often set below ground level. These arteries separate vehicles from pedestrians, keeping the city's green areas at one remove from the noise and pollution of the internal combustion engine, while also allowing through traffic to move at speeds that aren't possible on conventional city streets.

In one way, the Ville Radieuse idea has something in common with the Garden City movement that had begun thirty years earlier. There was the same concern to set people's homes among greenery, to bring something of the countryside into city life. But Le Corbusier's plan was actually completely different from celebrated English garden cities such as Letchworth or Welwyn. The English cities are low-rise and low density – the houses sprawl across the land and are set along curving streets that try to recreate the randomness of rural roads and villages. Ville Radieuse, by contrast, is high-rise and high density, and the roads are straight. The whole thing looks much more planned and controlled.

There is a more profound difference, too. The Garden City is inspired by individualism – each person or family lives in their own house (often semi-detached), with its own garden, separated from its neighbours by wooden fencing or a hedge. Corbusier's city, on the other hand, is a collective community. People live in apartments and share communal open space.

Although Ville Radieuse was not built, it was influential. The notion of separating vehicles and pedestrians was pioneered in North America in mostly low-density developments in the 1930s. Ville Radieuse showed how it could work in a high-density city, with a mix of tall buildings and green spaces. Hundreds of towns were replanned using this principle after the Second World War. All over the world planners of the 1950s and 1960s showed how the theory could work in practice. The idea of combining high-rise blocks with park-like green spaces also appealed, and was taken up in developments such as the Alton estate in Roehampton, southwest London. And in a few places Le Corbusier himself got the chance to build individual blocks that, in larger numbers, would have been the basis of the Ville Radieuse. The Unité d'habitation, Marseilles – a kind of vertical village of apartments, shops, crèche and hotel – survives to show how the vision might have worked.

APARTMENTS ON BRIDGES

Harvey Wiley Corbett and Hugh Ferriss, 1925

A Vision for a Metropolis of the Future

In 1925, the owners of Wanamaker's department store in
New York City, established since the late nineteenth century
and known as a retailer of beautiful and sophisticated goods
from all over the world, decided to hold an exhibition to
attract publicity. The theme was modern city design and
the title, 'Titan City: A Pictorial Prophecy of New York
1929–2026', gave a clue as to the scale of the architecture
and the ambition of the display. The architect Harvey
Wiley Corbett and the artist Hugh Ferriss, who had been
collaborating for a while on futuristic illustrations of city
buildings, especially skyscrapers, jumped at the chance this
offered. 'I think this is a most interesting opportunity',
writes Corbett, 'to get someone to pay for the futuristic
ideas we have discussed.'

Ferriss must have agreed. He had ten years' experience in
New York City as a freelance architectural illustrator, had
honed his own style and would have seen the exhibition as
a major job that could bring him publicity. Several artists
and architects were involved in the exhibition, and Corbett
and Ferriss played a major role. The show featured models
of buildings designed by Corbett. There were also a number
of Ferriss's illustrations, in his atmospheric, finely painted,
shadow-clouded style.

This was the period when American cities were growing
rapidly and many Americans began to see their ideal home
as somewhere in the town rather than on a patch of land in the
country. American architects and planners started to address
seriously how they could improve and beautify cities. They
embraced high-rise with enthusiasm, and competed to build
the tallest skyscraper. At the same time, they developed the
setback, the layout in which a building gets narrower higher
up, allowing sunlight to get to the streets below. So skyscrapers
dominated Ferriss's illustrations for the Titan City, but there
were also other self-consciously modern features such as
mooring points for airships and a recent idea for building
development: apartments set on bridges.

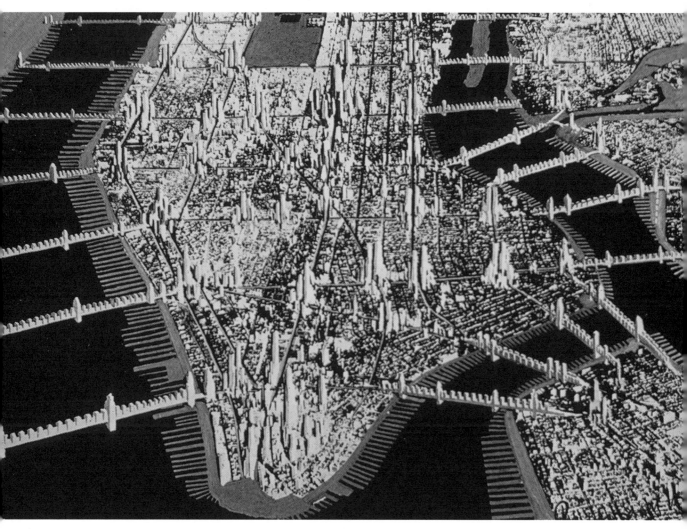

The notion of putting accommodation – either dwellings or offices – on a bridge is an old one: medieval and Renaissance cities often had buildings with shops and houses. The idea's revival seems to have begun with the architect Raymond Hood. He saw that cities such as New York were filling up fast – even the space for skyscrapers was limited, especially on a crowded island such as Manhattan. But the fact that Manhattan was surrounded by water was an opportunity – constructing more bridges could not only improve transport but also increase the available living space. So Ferriss, following in Hood's footsteps, drew a scaled-up suspension bridge in which the two towers are skyscrapers full of apartments, and apartments also spread out onto the span of the bridge, filling the area between the suspension chains and the bridge deck, while still allowing space for traffic to move across.

An aerial view of Manhattan shows the large number of bridges intended – and suggests the enormous housing capacity that would be provided.

The effect is bizarre, transforming a suspension bridge, usually a rather insubstantial-looking structure, into a solid and rather lumpy object. It looks an unlikely piece of engineering: the balancing of forces involved, not to mention the provision for expansion and contraction to cope with outside temperature changes, seem daunting to say the least. But both Hood and Ferriss claimed that the design could work structurally. In his proposals for New York, Hood presented a plan of Manhattan with the whole island ringed with apartment bridges. Spreading the city out across the Hudson and East rivers was an audacious concept to say the least. It would have taken many years to construct, even if it could be made to work.

The Titan City exhibition proved successful, both in attracting people to Wanamaker's store and in stimulating architects to think more about city design. Ferriss developed his ideas in further drawings. He believed passionately that his role as an architectural artist was not only to illustrate the ideas of architects, but also to show those architects how architecture could

Ferris's drawings of the proposed bridges showcase his drawing style with its highly atmospheric rendering of light and shade.

develop further. He tried to put this into practice in a book, *The Metropolis of Tomorrow*, which was published in 1929.

In *The Metropolis of Tomorrow*, Ferriss returns to the idea of Apartments on Bridges, with another illustration. There is enough detail in this to pick out individual windows and to get an idea of the building's gargantuan scale: the towers alone, at fifty or sixty floors each, are enormous – more than half the height of the Empire State, for example, which was to become the world's tallest building when construction finished two years after Ferriss's publication. Much more accommodation is ranged between the towers and on the short approach spans at either end of the bridge.

Ferriss's drawings are very powerful. They rely on strong contrast, with buildings shining out in white against a dark sky, or looming darkly against a pale background. They are not always finely detailed – the effect is often rather like a soft-focus photograph. But they give a very strong sense of the shape and form of buildings – skyscrapers especially – and of their gigantic scale.

Ferriss points out the advantages in his accompanying text: 'At first glance it would appear that such a location for office or residence is unusually desirable as to exposure, light and air. We may naturally assume landing stages, at the bases of the towers, for launch, yacht and hydroplane – whence it would be only a minute by elevator, to one's private door.' He also adds a note of humour, recalling that 'facetious minds' have alleged that the apartments might make domestic life bizarre or even dangerous: 'On the other hand, serious minds have claimed that the project is not only structurally sound but possesses unusual advantages, financially.' However, the construction costs would have been vast, even if the watery real estate on which the bridges were built was cheaper than anywhere on New York's streets or avenues.

Hood's and Ferriss's bizarre idea was unlikely ever to be constructed once, let alone in the numbers proposed by Hood in his map of Manhattan. However, the design still has its admirers, as much as anything because of the power of Ferriss's illustrations. His work has been impressing people since it first appeared in the 1920s. An article in the British *Architects' Journal* in 1927 sang his praises: 'Hugh Ferriss stands unequalled in his power to evoke the immediacy, the largeness, the ultimate sanity of great modern architecture. North Americans may well be proud of him.'

BERLIN, GERMANY

TOTAL THEATRE
Walter Gropius and Erwin Piscator, 1927

An Immersive Theatre, Designed to 'Surprise and Assault' the Spectator

The clash of egos, particularly between those of architect and client, can be a creative or destructive force in architecture. When an architect engages deeply with the client's needs and tastes, while also bringing something uniquely their own to the drawing board, the result can be magical. But two powerful personalities with irreconcilable differences can tear a project apart. And these are not mutually exclusive scenarios. Sometimes, conflict can engender magic and then destroy it.

Two of the plans prepared by Gropius show alternative arrangements of the stage: a centre stage (BELOW LEFT) and a stage at one end of the auditorium (BELOW RIGHT).

Walter Gropius and Erwin Piscator came together to create a new kind of theatre in the late 1920s. Gropius was one of the most influential figures in twentieth-century architecture. He was the founder of the famous German Bauhaus school, which transformed thinking about design in the early twentieth century and was one of the creators of architectural Modernism. Piscator was among the outstanding theatre directors of the period, an exponent of epic theatre with strong dramatic and political ideas. He wanted a new theatre building in which his ideas about a more immersive kind of drama, which enveloped the audience, could be made flesh and where the latest technology was available, including film projections, which he often used in his theatrical productions.

Gropius was in many ways the ideal architect for the job. He was fascinated by the theatre, and had seen how powerful theatrical events could be at the Bauhaus, where innovative ballet and other productions were staged. He had also been impressed by the theatrical ideas of his Bauhaus colleagues László Moholy-Nagy and Oskar Schlemmer. Schlemmer created revolutionary ballets at the Bauhaus, while Moholy-Nagy wrote intriguingly about a 'theatre of totality' that combined space, light, sound and movement. Moholy-Nagy described how a theatre might have hanging balcony-stages or bridges that could be moved around, bringing the actors very close to the audience and breaking down barriers between auditorium and stage. Notions such as these, involving elements of a building that could move or adapt in different ways, were a stimulating challenge to Gropius.

By spring 1927, the architect was working out these ideas on paper. The project became known as the Total Theatre, after the complete, immersive experience it would produce, and it conformed to no single template of theatre design. Instead of a fixed proscenium arch or apron stage, Gropius devised a movable stage with several different configurations: a proscenium; an amphitheatre arrangement in which the audience seating is wrapped around a thrust stage rather as in an ancient Greek theatre; and a setup with a central round stage with the audience completely surrounding it.

Around the auditorium there run a number of passageways in which movable platforms can travel, so that specific scenes can take place to one side, or at the back or very close to the audience. These platforms can also house musicians, adding a surround sound effect to the theatrical mix. And, as Piscator requested, film is a major element too, with the provision for numerous projection screens around the auditorium.

The effect of all this was not just to surround and immerse the audience, but also to give the impression of dissolving the architecture. Instead of the usual familiar parts of a theatre building – balconies, circles, boxes, proscenium arches, Baroque or Classical decoration – there was the all-embracing dramatic experience. As Gropius himself puts it: 'The division between acting and the audience no longer exists. Words, light and music no longer have a set place. The director becomes sovereign and dictates the course of the audience's interest according to the changing needs of the play.' Gropius encloses the resulting immersive space in an oval building with, in some versions of the plan, a domed roof. There are stair towers around the periphery and a service building with backstage facilities on one side.

The design went through several iterations, but in a matter of months Gropius had a version that pleased Piscator, who was busy getting together funds to build it. Then there was a delay, caused mainly by the fact that the hoped-for site proved too small and the search for land had to begin again.

At around this point, the ego clash seems to have started. Piscator wrote an enthusiastic account of the plans for the theatre, very much putting his own role in the foreground and implying that Gropius had merely 'assisted' him to create the plans. Gropius took offence at this. This was perhaps partly due to a thin skin, although Gropius did have a point. He was the architect, and he had spent a long time before the project began absorbing ideas about the theatre, especially at the Bauhaus. The project was as much his as Piscator's. Yet the architect's reaction was rather extreme: he took out patents on his design – which meant that he effectively divorced himself from Piscator, losing his main chance of getting the theatre built. He did try applying the design to other contexts and locations, but unsuccessfully.

Perhaps Gropius's inability to build his theatre for another client showed a failing similar to Piscator's. Just as the director downplayed the architect's role, so Gropius wrote Piscator out of the script. What both forgot was that collaboration was of the essence for the project and that the design, although highly adaptable, was made for a specific context. Few other clients wanted precisely this kind of theatre, and other directors had just as strong views as Piscator about the kind of building in which

they wanted to work. The project could only have been completed if the two prime movers had carried on working together.

Ideas about movable stages and designs that broke away from the proscenium arch remained in the air. The ninety years since Gropius and Piscator launched their project have seen countless new theatres with thrust stages, amphitheatre arrangements, 'in the round' staging or combinations of these. These are not due only to the influence of Gropius's Total Theatre. Similar ideas were espoused by other architects and directors, but the collaboration between Gropius and Piscator, together with their sad falling out, was a vital part of this movement.

Seating on three levels, with tightly curving circle and balcony as shown in the model, ensures that the entire audience is close to the action, however the auditorium is configured.

CHICAGO, USA

AERIAL RESTAURANT

Norman Bel Geddes, 1933

A Slowly Revolving Building Poised High Above Chicago's Exhibition Site

The American designer Norman Bel Geddes is best known as the creator of streamlined railway engines, automobiles and all kinds of machines and gadgets from weighing scales to radios, but he was not afraid to branch out into different areas of design. The 1920s was a pivotal decade for Bel Geddes. He did a lot of theatre work – directing plays as well as designing sets and theatre buildings. He worked on exhibition designs and advertising displays. And, in 1927, he announced that he would concentrate most of his attention on industrial design. In a few years, he had become one of America's most prominent industrial designers and had acquired a reputation as someone with a clear vision of a future in which technology would play a leading role. His work, with its bright colours, streamlined shapes and new materials, was soon known as the last thing in modernity.

All of Bel Geddes's talents came together in the work he did for various major exhibitions, including the Chicago Century of Progress Exhibition, or World's Fair, of 1933–4. These large-scale events drew numerous futuristic schemes from Bel Geddes, none more striking and forward-looking than the Aerial Restaurant he designed for the Chicago exhibition.

One of the things that the organizers of the World's Fairs liked about Bel Geddes was his theatricality – he believed not only that the exhibits should entertain and thrill visitors but that the structures that housed them should do so too. He wanted architecture – especially buildings connected with entertainment – to be alive, to engage people, and he wrote that 'unquestionably a new liveliness is coming into architecture… It can certainly be made as vivacious as the tabloids, the talkies, or vaudeville.'

Bel Geddes designed star-shaped theatres, theatres with curving forms drawing on the visual language of Art Deco, and all kinds of lavish restaurants. They were certainly lively and engaging, but Bel Geddes was not interested only in shape and surface. He was also driven to make his buildings work functionally. Mindful of the fact that everyone wants to eat at

roughly the same time, he was at pains to make dining rooms as spacious as possible, especially in exhibition complexes where choice of restaurant was limited. He wanted his buildings to be easy for staff to use too, with well-planned kitchens and adequate space and facilities for serving. And he wanted dining to be fun, and restaurant architecture to contribute to that; novel or unusual designs engaged diners – and enticed them inside.

All Bel Geddes's restaurant designs for the World's Fair were spectacular. The Island Dance Restaurant was to be built on a series of islands in one of Lake Michigan's lagoons; the

The clearest evidence for how the restaurant structure was designed is this model. The three dining floors are segments of a circle, ensuring that they do not cast continuous shadows on the windows of the lower levels and giving diners a mixture of sunshine and shade.

Bel Geddes created Futurama, a city set twenty years in the future, for the 1939 New York World's Fair. Expressways, allowing the rapid movement of large volumes of traffic, were a key part of the concept.

Aquarium Restaurant was to have walls that incorporated vast fish tanks. In many ways, the most spectacular was the Aerial Restaurant, which consists of a series of stacked, semicircular floors mounted on a tower and looking out over the exhibition grounds. The most surprising and modern thing about the building is that the whole structure revolves slowly, giving diners an ever-changing view as they enjoy their meals.

All three of the restaurant's floors are supported high in the air on a tower that made the structure equivalent in height to a twenty-five-storey building. The lowest level (still more than halfway up the tower) holds a restaurant and dance floor that accommodates 600 people. Above this is the middle level, which was designed to serve light refreshments at budget prices to around 400. On top is a smaller, high-class restaurant that could seat 200. The kitchens are in a basement, and Bel Geddes planned nine elevators to send food up to the restaurant floors; the tower also contains three elevators for the diners.

The building met the needs of the situation well, providing plenty of space and the added benefit of a viewing platform, all of which took up very little ground space. That was impressive, but what really engaged people who saw the plans was the fact that the restaurant revolved. This alone brought it strong support when the exhibition committee discussed which of the many plans submitted would be accepted.

The committee even turned a visual challenge into an opportunity. How would you decorate such a high-tech building and make it inviting? Answer: you didn't need to; it was intriguing enough as a piece of naked engineering. People knew that engineering feats fascinated people – from London's Crystal Palace of 1851 to Paris's Eiffel Tower of 1889, they had drawn people into exhibitions and kept them talking long afterwards. The Aerial Restaurant promised to be another such draw – something that people would travel a long way to see.

So why was the project not built? Bel Geddes submitted many ideas for the exhibition, and it seems extraordinary that one of the most eye-catching was rejected. One reason is that the budget got suddenly tight because the lead-up to the exhibition coincided with the Wall Street crash of 1929. Another may have been prejudice against the designer. The architectural establishment was sometimes suspicious of Bel Geddes because he was not trained as a professional architect. He made his living as an industrial designer, a teacher and in a variety of other design jobs, but he was not qualified to practise architecture. This was almost certainly a major problem for some of the committee members, although it would have been possible for a qualified architect to develop Bel Geddes's plans and see them to fruition. In addition, several members of the committee were high-profile architects, including Raymond Hood and, in the early stages of the planning, Frank Lloyd Wright, and they supported him but did not prevail.

To have the idea for the restaurant turned down was only a temporary setback for Bel Geddes. He carried on designing everything from cars to cocktail shakers. He publicized his work in books such as *Horizons* (1932), which spread the word about streamlining, and *Magic Motorways* (1940), which advocated an interstate highway system. He even had popular success in the exhibition world at the New York World's Fair of 1939, when his Futurama exhibit showed a model of a future city with improved traffic circulation.

The Aerial Restaurant seemed like the future too, but it is now known mainly from a model made by Maurice Goldberg, photographs of which have been catching people's eyes since they were first published soon after Bel Geddes did the design. Its influence lingered on in other futuristic structures, especially revolving restaurants such as the one that helped make London's BT Tower famous or the one at the Ala Moana Center in Honolulu, both 1960s structures. Buildings are meant to stand still, but the idea that they could also move has never quite gone away.

LIVERPOOL, UK
CATHOLIC CATHEDRAL
Sir Edwin Lutyens, 1930–3

A Cavernous Domed Church for Liverpool's Large Catholic Community

Since the middle of the nineteenth century, when many Irish Catholics moved there after the famine of 1848, Liverpool has had a large Catholic population. By 1853, the Catholic Church decided the city needed a cathedral, and Edward Welby Pugin was commissioned to design one in the grounds of a Catholic school, St Edward's College, in Everton. Pugin, architect of many Catholic churches, was the son of the more famous A. W. N. Pugin (joint architect of the Houses of Parliament) and like his father he believed that the Gothic style was the one most appropriate for churches. For many people, the pointed-arched Gothic style was the best way of making an architectural connection with the 'true' faith of the Middle Ages, when England was a Catholic country. For Liverpool, Pugin designed a large Gothic cathedral with a tall spire. This building was begun, but only the Lady Chapel was completed when the church decided to concentrate its resources and money on helping the poor, with the result that the building project was put on hold.

Lutyens's design produces an impression of massiveness – quite different from the airy Gothic style of the medieval cathedrals and of the Catholic cathedral proposed for Liverpool in the nineteenth century.

In 1922, the plan to build a cathedral was revived, in part as a result of a move to construct a memorial to Archbishop Thomas Whiteside, who had died the previous year. This time, there was to be a more central location, and the Church bought a suitable plot of land, the site of a former workhouse on Brownlow Hill, near the middle of the city. There was then another pause, during which Archbishop Frederick William Keating and his successor Richard Downey raised funds. Enthusiasm for the project increased, especially in 1929. This was a year of celebration, marking the hundredth anniversary of the Roman Catholic Relief Act, which had removed many of the restrictions that had been placed on British Catholics since the Reformation. By this point, there was sufficient backing and Sir Edwin Lutyens was chosen as architect.

Lutyens, whose most famous structures were the Cenotaph in Whitehall and the Viceroy's Palace in New Delhi, was a very different kind of architect from Pugin. Unencumbered by Gothic or religious baggage, he was experienced in designing in many different styles while bringing his own individual vision to each. Many believe him to be both the most versatile and the greatest British architect of the period. For the new cathedral at Liverpool, Lutyens chose the Byzantine style, with a central dome and a barrel-vaulted interior. Byzantine architecture, which originated in the eastern Roman empire, was most closely associated with the Orthodox churches. However, it also had many Catholic enthusiasts, particularly since the late nineteenth century, when Britain's foremost Catholic cathedral, at Westminster, was built in this style.

Lutyens was determined to make a contrast with the city's Anglican cathedral, a sandstone Gothic building with a great tower, which was then under construction. The materials are a contrast, too – pinkish brick and silver-grey Irish granite. But the main quality that distinguishes Lutyens's design is its sheer size. The dome is 168ft (51m) in diameter and the lantern above it rises to a height of 520ft (158m); internally, the height is 300ft (91m). This made the dome even larger than the one crowning St Peter's in Rome and, as a whole, the cathedral was to be the second-largest church in the world. Lutyens not only wanted to contrast with the Anglican cathedral, but also to upstage it.

Conscious of the amount of money still to raise, Lutyens suggested that a large wood and plaster model of the building should be made to inspire fresh interest in the grand project.

The model, built by John Thorp, is at a scale of 1:48 and, at 13ft (4m) high and 17ft (5.2m) long, is something of a show-stopper in itself. Its very presence helped garner publicity for the project, and the public profile of the building became even higher when the plans were shown at the Royal Academy Summer Exhibition in 1932. The reaction was stunned and positive. Writing in *Country Life*, Christopher Hussey was enthusiastic: 'When erected the cathedral must be one of the wonders of the world, and one that none but the genius of this particular architect could have conceived.'

The model proved a useful fundraising tool. Because it is so large, people can actually get inside it, and, fitted with details such as cast-metal statues, it gives a clear impression of the majestic and awe-inspiring architecture of the interior.

Construction work began in June 1933. Building even the foundations was a major task and, by 1941, only the crypt had been completed when funding dwindled and the war put a stop to further work. By the time the Second World War was over, the estimated cost had risen from the original £3 million to close on £30 million and Lutyens had died, in 1944. These were not the only difficulties: in 1945, the priority was to rebuild the houses and other essential buildings that had been damaged by enemy bombardment, and Liverpool, as a major port, had been heavily bombed. Even the Anglican cathedral

This rapid sketch by Lutyens shows how he tried variants on the basic design of a Byzantine-style cathedral with a large dome. Here he included a pair of towers and an additional smaller dome.

Lutyens's drawing shows an interior of thick walls pierced by semicircular arches opening out into a large space beneath the dome, which is hinted at on the right-hand side of the paper.

had taken a hit in one of its transepts. The builders did not return to the Catholic cathedral site.

In 1953, Archbishop Downey, who had commissioned the cathedral, died, and his successor looked at the plans again. The plan's ambitious scale and the huge rise in costs meant that people began to rethink the project. Some thought that it might be possible to complete the cathedral on a smaller scale, so Adrian Gilbert Scott, son of Giles Gilbert Scott, the architect of the Anglican cathedral, was brought in to produce a new set of plans. He proposed a smaller building, still with a large dome, on the existing foundations. However, the revised design did not win wide support and was laid aside.

The early 1960s saw another new start, this time with a Modernist design by Sir Frederick Gibberd, again on the same site above Lutyens's crypt. This is the design that finally went ahead, with Consecration in 1967, giving Liverpool a Catholic cathedral at last. The distinctive, circular design of Gibberd, which has an unusual, funnel-like shape, is far smaller than the building that Lutyens had planned. Yet its distinctive form is still memorable and, to many, inspiring. However, it will never be a true equivalent to the vast monument proposed by Lutyens, which would have been an enduring beacon for Catholics and a true counterpart to the great Anglican cathedral facing it at the other end of the city's Hope Street.

THE ILLINOIS

Frank Lloyd Wright, 1959

A Mile-High Skyscraper in Downtown Chicago

After the race to build the world's tallest tower became big
news in the 1920s, more and more architects wanted to build
skyscrapers – for an ambitious architect, the chance to create
a tall tower in a major city could bring fame like nothing else.
Even for an experienced architect who did not need to prove
anything, such a project could be tempting. In 1959, Frank
Lloyd Wright was one of the most experienced designers in the
business. Already in his nineties and, as it turned out, in the last
year of his life, he was known all over the world. And he was
not slowing up: that year, he proposed the tallest skyscraper
anyone had ever dared to imagine.

Wright is probably the most celebrated of all American
architects. Over his long career he designed all kinds of
buildings, but was famous above all for his houses. The best
known of these are low-slung and seem to sprawl across their
sites, but when you look closely at them they are beautifully
planned, and the apparent sprawl is a way of making best
use of the site and space, and integrating the house into the
landscape via verandas, terraces, pergolas and similar features
that blur the boundary between indoors and out.

For Wright, it seemed, the ideal way for an American to
live was in a house surrounded by a sizeable garden. One of his
most cherished projects was a town that he called Broadacre
City, which he published in a book in 1932. This was a large
urban plan made up mostly of 1 acre (0.4ha) plots with a
house on each. Transport was mainly by car and apartments
were few. It was called a city but was really a suburb, and
Wright saw it, in the 1920s and early 1930s, as a blueprint for
American life.

Wright was serious about Broadacre City. He even had an
enormous model made of it. But by 1959 he had acknowledged
that not everyone could live in a suburb with 1 acre (0.4ha) of
land, and he was looking at more intensely urban communities.
By this time he had designed a number of tall buildings and
had become interested in the skyscraper. Wright, never short
of nerve and never afraid of a grand gesture, decided to design

OPPOSITE *In Wright's coloured
perspective drawing, the mile-
high skyscraper pierces stylized
clouds that trail diagonally across
the paper. Even at this scale, there
is not much scope for showing fine
detail at the foot of the enormous
tower* (INSET).

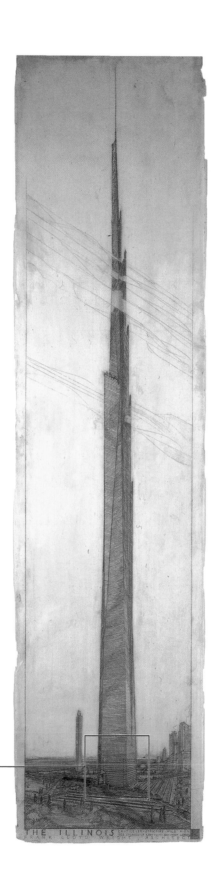

THE ILLINOIS

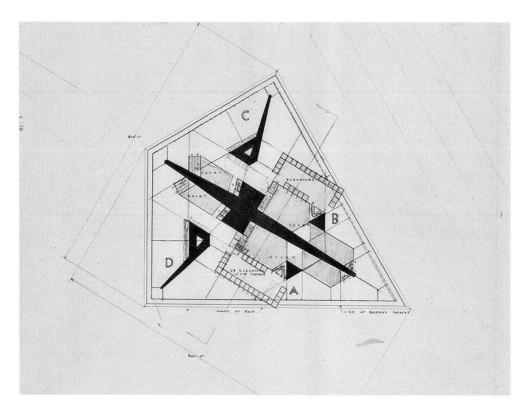

the tallest skyscraper ever conceived, something bigger than anything currently existing or planned and four times the height of the Empire State, then the world's tallest building. Wright's plan was for a skyscraper 1 mile (1.6km) high.

Skyscrapers were the great American architectural invention. They began in the USA, in Chicago, and it was the USA that had the most celebrated examples: New York's glorious Art Deco Chrysler Building and the Empire State, which had been the world's tallest building since it was collated in 1931. Wright proposed to build his 1 mile- (1.6km-) high tower in Chicago, the 'home' of the skyscraper and also the city where he had begun his own practice as an architect and which was home to some of his best-known buildings.

Chicago has some outstanding architecture, but it had never seen anything like Wright's tower, which he called The Illinois. The figures are astonishing: 528 floors, 18.46 million sq. ft (1.71 million sq. m) of floor space, seventy-six elevators, parking for 15,000 cars. Some estimates put the number of people using the building, either working or living there, at 100,000. The shape was unprecedented: a tapering form, rather like a jagged-edged or multifaceted spire. It would have looked stunning: acres of glass glinting in the sunshine, miles of gold-coloured

The shape of the tower varies as it rises. This floor plan shows a kite-shaped level, revealing how Wright made the building streamlined to reduce wind resistance.

metal. Wright produced an impressive drawing of it extending into the clouds and dwarfing the rest of Chicago. This artwork, itself 22ft (6.7m) high, rendered many viewers speechless.

The Illinois's structure is based on a triangular plan and a tripod-like framework of steel that was designed for stability. This form was also an answer to a big question with any tall building: high winds can make skyscrapers shake. Wright argued that the tripod structure would minimize the effects of this wind load, preventing the feelings of nausea that affect people at the top of tall structures that wobble.

Impressive as it looked, the tower posed major questions of its own. Could mid-century technology produce elevators that were efficient enough to service such a tall structure? Yes, it could, argued Wright, who proposed that some of the elevators in his building should be atomic-powered. These nuclear-powered beasts are themselves five storeys high, so that they could service five levels at a time; they could carry 1200 people at a time. They probably did not seem overly far-fetched in 1959, when technologists were predicting atomic-powered boats and cars in the not-so-distant future.

How would the enormous number of people using the building get there? And how would their food and other needs arrive? By road, mostly, seemed to be the answer, hence the number of parking places, though the architect also wanted to include landing and parking facilities for 150 helicopters.

Wouldn't such a large number of vehicles converging on one spot need lots of new roads? Yes, came the response: an area of downtown Chicago would have to be razed to the ground to service the tower. And that was not necessarily a bad thing, argued advocates of the skyscraper. Part of the point of stacking dwellings and offices in the air was that it freed up the ground. Some of the space could be used for parks and gardens. But with a tower 1 mile (1.6km) high, a lot of the surrounding ground would be covered with tarmac.

Even today, with buildings such as Dubai's Burj Khalifa (2723ft/830m to its tip) finished and more tall towers on the way, we are nowhere near Wright's 1 mile- (1.6km-) high ambition. But some recent towers are looking more and more like The Illinois. London's celebrated Shard, at 1017ft (310m) a mere junior compared to The Illinois, has enough of the tapering shape of Wright's design to look like a descendant. Burj Khalifa itself has the tapering profile and triangular plan. It is almost as if the future envisioned in 1959 is beginning to take shape.

NEW NORCIA

Pier Luigi Nervi, 1957

A Monastery and Pilgrimage Centre for the Benedictine Order

Throughout the twentieth century, buildings got more and more structurally complex and daring. This exploration of new kinds of forms and structures has meant that close collaboration between architects and engineers is crucial. Engineers are the people who make it possible to construct innovative buildings, who know the capabilities of materials and who can do the mathematics necessary to ensure that everything will stand up and stay standing up. But engineers work in the background. Most people could name an architect or two; few could come up with the name of a single civil engineer. Yet now and then an engineer becomes well known, and this is sometimes because they take a key role in shaping a building's outer appearance as well as its inner structure. Such a figure was the great Italian engineer Pier Luigi Nervi.

Nervi made his name in the interwar period, and by the 1950s was working on prominent buildings such as the UNESCO headquarters in Paris and the graceful Pirelli Tower in Milan. He developed a special expertise in concrete shell structures, and by this period was working internationally, in the USA and Latin America as well as in Europe. In 1957, he was commissioned to work on an Australian project – a monastery at New Norcia, Perth.

New Norcia had been established, northeast of Perth, as a Benedictine settlement in 1847. The name derives from the founder of the Benedictine order, St Benedict of Nursia (San Benedetto da Norcia in Italian), after the name of the saint's home town in Perugia. There had been plans to build a new cathedral there between the world wars, but the Second World War had put everything on hold.

Then, in 1951, the monastery was chosen as one of the stops on a Catholic pilgrimage, the peace tour of the statue of the Lady of Fatima. This was a worldwide tour, during which Catholic priests carried the Portuguese statue to numerous European countries, as well as to India and Australia, leading prayers for world peace as they did so. This event attracted

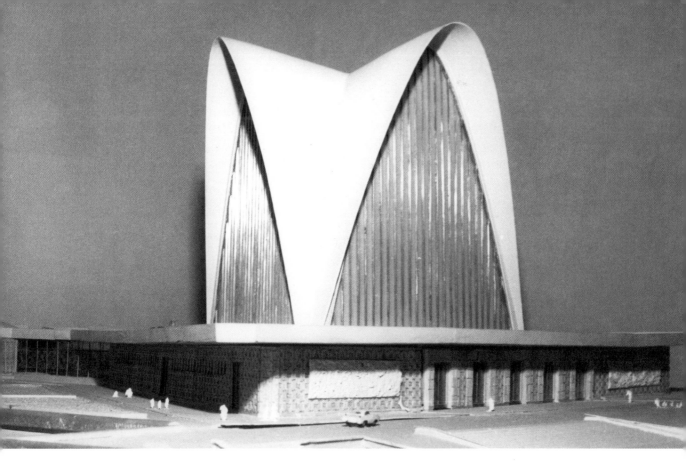

large crowds at most of its stopping places, and at New Norcia there were too many people to fit into the existing church. The pilgrimage was followed in the same year by the appointment of a new abbot, Gregory Gomez. Again, the celebrations and services had to be held outdoors. Abbot Gomez decided that a new, larger church was needed.

For help in choosing an architect, the abbot went to the Catholic Church's Institute for Liturgical Art and they recommended the team of architect Carlo Vannoni and engineer Pier Luigi Nervi. They would have known Nervi's previous work for the Church at a Benedictine abbey in Minnesota and at the pilgrimage centre of Lourdes, France, among other places. The underground basilica at Lourdes, which has a vast space covered by a series of shallow concrete arches, must have especially impressed the Institute – his experience with this building would have made Nervi a natural choice.

The design that Nervi and Vannoni came up with was still more dramatic than Lourdes. The cathedral has an unusual, three-pronged plan, with the High Altar at the centre. Each of the three fronts is dominated by a tall parabolic arch infilled

This model shows how, above the ground-floor level, the church design is dominated by the parabolic roofs and the enormous windows beneath them.

with an enormous stained-glass window, and the three arches together make up a lantern or cupola some 100ft (30m) tall. The bases of the three arches form an equilateral triangle, and beneath this and in the surrounding lower spaces is seating for 820 people and standing room for a further thousand. The structure of the arches is of reinforced concrete. Their exact proportion and details were worked out by Nervi, whose calculations defined their elegant shape. As well as the cathedral, the team designed a three-storey monastery with cells for more than a hundred monks, together with ancillary rooms and guest accommodation.

The unusual triangular form of the cathedral had various sources. As well as the obvious symbolism of the Holy Trinity, Nervi may have been inspired by the cave with a triangular opening at Subiaco, in which St Benedict lived as a hermit. The parabolic arches and corresponding shell roofs of the church were motifs that were especially dear to Nervi – he had used similar forms in aircraft hangars; parabolas are also seen in his building for St Louis Abbey, St Louis, Missouri, and paraboloid arches would appear later is his design for St Mary's Cathedral, San Francisco.

The engineer was at least as responsible for the striking appearance of the cathedral and monastery as the architect Vannoni. Nervi was known to encourage his engineering colleagues to set at least as much store by the appearance of their buildings as the all-important structural calculations. So at New Norcia, Nervi was responsible for both the engineering and architecture of the key element of the project – the cathedral – while Vannoni did the designs for the monastery. His hand is clear in the great parabolic shells of the cathedral. Nervi had developed expertise in these shell structures in buildings such as his famous Palazetto dello Sport, the small stadium in Rome used during the 1960 Olympics. However, Nervi was based in Italy, far away from the site, and the project also had the vital input of an Australian engineer, George Hondros. Hondros assured Nervi that the builders of Western Australia would be able to construct his novel building, although, even so, Nervi considered having the parabolic concrete arches prefabricated in Europe and shipped to the site.

In the event, this decision did not have to be made. Although the project was begun, it quickly became clear that the amount of money needed was too high to be realistic. The building project was abandoned in the early 1960s. Only the plans and models remain – and the vast stained-glass windows, which were made in Italy before the project was halted and are said to be in storage. Nervi went on to do further work in Australia, including the prominent, tall, round tower called Australia Square, in Sydney. His reputation as an innovative engineer remains, confirmed both by such completed buildings and the unrealized plan for New Norcia.

A Christ in Majesty design for a stained-glass window takes full advantage of the height of the parabola.

CHAPTER 6
MOVING ON

The crushing pressures faced by through the second half of the twentieth century…

… and into the twenty-first, but with the difference that the changes come faster. One response has been to build ever-larger structures to house city dwellers, their workplaces, leisure facilities and services: such megastructures – buildings the size of an entire towns – were born. These promised to address urban problems at a stroke – to accommodate people, to reduce transport times and costs by placing homes and workplaces close to each other, to rationalize transport routes, to separate people from the noise and pollution of roads or railways. Thus, a megastructure could be an ideal city in a single structure.

However, such large-scale projects were both expensive and unwieldy. With the rate of change speeding up so much, they could be outdated before they were completed. Hence the desire to look at building anew, and to build in adaptability. Arata Isozaki's tree-like Clusters in the Air, which allowed prefabricated modules to be added to its branches, is one example of flexibility. Perhaps the ultimate proposals for the flexible city came from British practice Archigram, which created designs such as the Plug-In City and the Walking City, founded on adaptability. Plans such as these needed all the resources of twentieth-century technology to look even remotely plausible.

the world's cities have continued

Isozaki's arboreal buildings and Archigram's insect-like moving structures suggested new sources for architecture in the natural world and were a world away from the white rectangular boxes produced by the Modernist architects. They were part of an opening up of architecture in the late twentieth century, an explosion of styles and approaches from High-tech to Postmodernism, from the angular forms of the Bangkok Hyperbuilding by Rem Koolhaas and Office for Metropolitan Architecture (OMA) to the curves of structures in Hong Kong by Zaha Hadid.

Buildings, large and small, also consume resources, and environmental pressures impacted on architecture and continue to do so. Ecological awareness can be present but invisible in architecture (a question of hidden insulation or reduced 'material miles') or clearly present as an obvious statement (a small, off-grid house equipped with everything from triple glazing to composting toilets). Can eco-architecture and large structures come together? Architects increasingly explore the possibility, and buildings such as Vincent Callebaut's Asian Cairns, combining farms with skyscrapers, is one daring attempt. Questioning current thinking, offering ideals, trying to make the future real: architectural projects continue to do these things as they did when Renaissance architects were dreaming up their ideal cities 500 years ago.

TOKYO BAY PLAN

Kenzo Tange, 1960

A Plan to Extend Japan's Capital Across Tokyo Bay

After the Second World War, Japan faced as big a task of regeneration and recovery as any of the combatant nations. The loss of life, the destruction caused by the atomic bombs on Hiroshima and Nagasaki, and the humiliation of defeat all left deep wounds. But by the 1950s and 1960s, the country was recovering, and a combination of government intervention, US presence and national resilience had led to the Japanese economy becoming the second largest in the world before 1970.

These developments posed challenges for architects and planners. A fast-growing economy meant fast-growing cities, but unchecked urban growth could bring its own problems. In many parts of the world, a situation such as this would result in urban sprawl – undisciplined and unplanned development extending for miles along arterial roads. In Japan, the local geography posed an added problem: because such a large proportion of Japan is mountainous, cities such as Tokyo were in danger of simply running out of land. By 1960, Tokyo was fast approaching a population of 10 million – a size that no city authorities had had to cope with before and which seemed to need a new approach to architecture and planning. Kenzo Tange, perhaps Japan's greatest post-war architect, had an answer. His 1960 Tokyo Bay Plan envisaged extending the city across the water of Tokyo Bay.

Tange's scheme had its roots in an architectural movement called Metabolism, which grew directly out of Japan's renewal of architecture after the war. The Metabolists advocated the organic growth of design and technology, mirroring the way in which life on Earth has developed organically, as their manifesto puts it 'from atom to nebula'. The Metabolists combined the design of megastructures with an element of organic growth. For example, they proposed buildings or cities with add-on or plug-in elements, that could be attached to the main body of the structure later to allow it to grow in a way that was both planned and responsive to changing needs.

One of the first Metabolist projects was a design known as Marine City or Ocean City (1958), by Kiyonori Kikutake.

OPPOSITE *From above, the overall structure of the plan is clear, with its linear core linking two sides of the bay and acting as the stem for a series of branches containing buildings.*

This was based on circles of development – some containing residential structures, some workplaces – that floated on the ocean. The circular platforms created what the Metabolists called 'artificial land', relieving the pressure on existing sites. They were also expandable – you could add further circles, or extend the structures on the original ones.

Tange took this idea of artificial land and applied it to Tokyo Bay. His plan consists of a series of structures stretching across the bay – not circles this time but centred on a linear spine with a series of smaller branches leading off it at right angles. Tange calls the spine the 'civic axis'. It leads out of the centre of Tokyo and stretches some 11 miles (18km) across the bay. It is designed to contain transport infrastructure, allowing cars and trains to travel rapidly before they branch off along smaller local routes to reach their destination.

The civic axis gives Tange's city a new kind of structure. Traditional cities are usually arranged around a central feature such as a square with routes radiating outwards. When the city grows, more and more buildings are added on the edges, increasing the flow of people in and out of the centre. So, while this arrangement works well for a small town, in a major city with a large number of commuters it results in traffic jams and strain on the transport system. By proposing a linear core Tange's Tokyo Bay development promised both to work better for transportation and to allow the organic growth of branches as required.

The axis is designed to accommodate both monorails and roads – together with parking for nearly a million cars. From the car parks and monorail stations, pedestrian pathways lead to squares and other areas where people can congregate. The axis also contains shopping centres and large office and administrative buildings, and Tange produced cross-sections showing how the axis can accommodate these structures at various different levels, creating plentiful artificial land out of the site.

The branches running at right angles to the civic axis are expressways leading to residential zones. These zones are partly set on reclaimed land, partly on piles above the water, and contain – as well as housing and car parking – facilities such as schools, local shops and kindergartens. Each small residential zone is served by a monorail station, and each set of buildings on its rectangular island or platform is grouped around a square. The architecture of these residential islands is striking, consisting of structures with sweeping upper surfaces with a slight concave curve, reflecting roofs in pagodas and other traditional Japanese buildings. The housing is set in these outer sweeping structures, to give natural light and views out across the bay, while the public facilities are housed inside and the car parking is tucked away below.

The plans of the scheme were developed in some detail, and the architect also supplied suggested costs indicating that, although revolutionary and conceived on a vast scale, the plan was a serious proposal that could be built. The fact that it made use of the bay, minimizing disruption to the rest of the city, also stood in its favour. However, it required a large budget and it also needed central planning – the Metabolists' grand ideas were impossible in a climate in which planning was largely left to private enterprise. For a while the plan seemed realizable, but for these reasons it did not get farther than Tange's elaborate presentation.

Although the original Tange plan came to nothing, it has remained well known to professionals, both as a key project in the career of one of Japan's great architects, and as a major example of a new kind of city plan that combines a radical, spinal approach with an organic view of growth and the idea of building over water. All these things make the plan rewarding for architects to study. Japanese planners, continually aware of the pressures on Tokyo's urban structure, have revisited its ideas more than once. Tange himself came back to the challenge posed by Japan's capital in 1986, and then Kisho Kurokawa prepared a 'New Tokyo Plan 2025'. Both of these plans use reclaimed land and floating architecture together. The influence of Tange's 1960 project has continued.

In the architect's model the complex traffic routes and extensive tall buildings in the central spine of the scheme are very clear. The buildings on the branches, with their pagoda-like roofs (upper right) can also be seen.

ENDLESS HOUSE

Frederick Kiesler, 1960

A Family House With a Truly Organic Design

In 1960, a model of a house was shown at New York's Museum
of Modern Art (MoMA), a model so extraordinary that it
was hardly recognizable as a building at all. It was called the
Endless House, and it was a structure without straight lines,
in which floors merged seamlessly into walls and walls into
ceilings, creating rounded, organic internal spaces that flowed
into one another. It was quite unlike the orthogonal buildings
that Americans were used to, and unlike any house most of the
visitors to the museum had seen. The design was by Frederick
Kiesler, an architect who had been born in what is now
Ukraine but had lived in the USA for almost forty years.

This 'new' way of designing a house was something that
Kiesler had been developing for many years – in a sense he
began work on it even before he moved to America. His
exploration of new ways of handling space dates back to
1925, when he produced a three-dimensional installation for
that year's Exposition Internationale des Arts Décoratifs et
Industriels Modernes in Paris, the exhibition that showcased a
range of contemporary decorative styles, from Dutch de Stijl to
French Art Deco. Kiesler's installation was called Raumstadt
(Space-City or City of Space) and was a large construction of
wood and canvas, about 66 × 33 × 26ft (20 × 10 × 8m). Based
on rectangles and straight lines, its open wooden framework
was painted white, and parts of the framework were filled in
with panels in red, blue or yellow.

The effect of this collection of planes and lines was rather
like a three-dimensional version of an abstract painting by
Mondrian, and it was suspended from the ceiling of the gallery
so that it seemed to be caught in mid-air. Its ostensible purpose
was to act as a support system for an exhibition display, but
Kiesler saw it as a model of a city, asymmetrical and free-
floating, and an exploration of 'free space' to create a place
without walls or foundations, a home for a modern society
where a new kind of society could grow and flourish. Although
Raumstadt was based on straight lines and right angles, Kiesler
was soon questioning this orthogonal approach, and rejecting

*With its rough surfaces, organic
forms and complete lack of
resemblance to conventional
buildings, Kiesler's Endless
House rewrites the architectural
rule book.*

most of the other accepted norms of architecture, too. 'No more walls!' he declared in a manifesto of 1925.

In the late 1920s, when he moved to New York, Kiesler devoted a lot of his time to work outside the usual run of architecture. He designed shop window displays, notably for Saks Fifth Avenue, and worked in the world of art gallery design, specifically with Peggy Guggenheim's Art of This Century Gallery. His work for Guggenheim was particularly provocative – his interior had curved walls and pictures that stuck out into the room, apparently a gesture of defiance to the Nazis, who had displayed paintings by so-called 'degenerate' artists (those who produced the modern art that the Nazis despised) at odd angles, in order to ridicule them. The work for Guggenheim also led Kiesler to do furniture designs, and some of the furniture he created for her – biomorphic tables and chairs that are all curves – leaves the straight-lined approach behind. By the late 1940s, he was exploring this kind of organic form on a larger scale, by creating an architecture of curves and developing buildings that no longer had identifiable components such as columns, roofs or floors.

What Kiesler wanted to do in architecture was revealed in a design proposal called the Space House. This was a spheroid or roughly egg-shaped structure, which the architect suggested should have a large, double-height living area in the middle and, towards the ends where the building was lower, private rooms for the various occupants. He saw this as an ideal layout for a building that would accommodate parents and children, where the generations needed both small, intimate spaces of their own and a larger, more generous, collective space, too. Bedrooms and a room such as a library, where someone could be alone with their thoughts, could be smaller rooms; living and dining rooms would be higher. According to this logic, the egg-shaped form 'grew' as the result of the spatial requirements of the users.

Kiesler's reasoning shows how he thought of the egg-like Space House in three dimensions from the outset. He rejected the idea, which he attributed to Functionalist or Modernist designers, that an architect should start with a floor plan and develop the design upwards from that. The floor plan, he argued, was the house's footprint, nothing more. We would get into trouble, argued Kiesler, if we tried to design a human being from a footprint – we would create a being that was all heels and toes. An architect has to look at the design in three dimensions from the start.

By 1960, when the MoMA exhibition came along, Kiesler was ready to extend his radical handling of space and make it more complex, while still basing it on real human needs. The Endless House model that he made for the show stands on a series of plinths or pylons that hold it well above the site. A curving staircase rises from ground level to the house itself, which consists of an elongated form, swelling in places and narrowing in others, and pierced with large, irregular openings, some roughly triangular, others rounded, one tear-shaped. The plaster surface of the model is rough, as if the structure is made of raw concrete, and the 'endless' quality comes from the continuous way in which one part of the building seems to merge into the next, with no formal facade, no front, no back and no ends.

The building looks odd and unfathomable, but Kiesler explained it clearly in terms of its function. It was designed as a family home for a couple and their children. The plans indicate distinct spaces: a large living room with a central fireplace in the middle of the house; a bedroom for the adults at one end of the building; the children's room at the other end, near the kitchen and dining area; tucked away to one side is a small quiet room; and staircases give access to different levels.

When they commissioned the Endless House design from Kiesler, the museum authorities and architect had hoped to build a full-size version of the house in MoMA's grounds. However, by the time the architect had got to work on the plans and model, the museum had begun a project to extend its own building, and there was no longer any space for a full-size Endless House. The building remained a project on paper and in plaster, and Kiesler died in 1965, too soon to find another site for his revolutionary structure.

CLUSTERS IN THE AIR

Arata Isozaki, 1962

Apartments 'Growing' in the Sky, Like the Leaves on a Tree

The Metabolist movement began in Japan at the end of the 1950s, in part as a response to the architectural challenges that the country faced after the Second World War. Leading lights of the movement included such major Japanese architects as Kenzo Tange and Kiyonori Kikutake, and among those to be deeply influenced by the Metabolists was Arata Isozaki. He trained with Tange at Tokyo University before working with his teacher and then starting his own practice, and so was at the heart of the new developments, although he was not an official member of the Metabolist group. In 1962, only two years after Tange's own ambitious Tokyo Bay Plan (see entry on page 194), Isozaki put forward his answer to the expanding Japanese city – Clusters in the Air.

Isozaki's project drew on a key principle of the Metabolist movement – that large-scale structures should be able to 'grow', both vertically and horizontally, and so architecture should no longer be guided by the old Modernist rule that 'form follows function'. This key Modernist notion depends on there being a definable function for a building. The Metabolists had noticed something about modern life that made them question this – the accelerating pace of change. The essential thing now was that structures should be able to adapt and grow in ways hardly predictable when they were first planned. Adaptability was one of the most important drivers of Metabolist architecture, and the one that made it apt to speak of this kind of building as organic. This approach to design was, therefore, a rejection of the Modernist orthodoxy in favour of something more flexible, while making full use of technological resources to create advanced structures.

The solution proposed by Isozaki was not to address the growth of the city by extending it over the sea, as in Tange's Tokyo Bay Plan, but by building upwards – and then outwards. So, in Clusters in the Air, Isozaki designed a tree-like structure, with a large, tall central core from which horizontal elements could 'grow' out, like branches. The

central cores or trunks are very large – they have to be strong enough to support enormous structures and also to house the elevators that make up the central transport network. The branches, although likewise huge, work on a more human scale. They are made up of prefabricated modules. Each module can play the role of an entire conventional building: for example, an individual house. Further modules can be added as needed, or reproduced to create additional 'trees', as the city grows or its needs evolve; or they can be replaced with different modules as people's needs change.

So, like Lissitzky's 'horizontal skyscrapers' (see Cloud Irons entry on page 152) on a much larger scale, the Clusters in the Air use relatively little ground space, but fit in an enormous amount of accommodation above ground level. As with the

Hundreds of small modules (INSET) are designed to attach to the tree-like structure, making the Clusters in the Air into highly flexible structures that can adapt with changing needs.

Cloud Irons, strategically spaced around the Moscow ring road, there were intended to be several Clusters – a forest rather than a single tree – giving the project potentially vast scale.

Where Lissitzky had designed blocks high above Moscow, Isozaki was proposing megastructures in the air. The cores that hold up these structures are designed both as massive supports and as vertical highways, delivering residents to the right level before they make their way along the horizontal axis to their modular apartments. The experience of living there would have been unlike life on the ground, or even in a conventional high-rise block.

The Clusters in the Air would have transformed the city where they were based, too. Although not necessarily taller than regular skyscrapers, their tree-like shape was totally different, and would have altered the whole visual effect of a city. It is not enough to say, as we do of skyscrapers, that they change the skyline – the Clusters would have replaced the skyline with something else, effectively a new city in the air.

Like Lissitzky before him, the advocates of these new urban megastructures hoped that they would revolutionize the cities where they were built. There was a conviction that modern cities needed a completely new urban pattern. The old, cluttered street patterns of many cities, from Europe to Japan, were under huge pressure – from traffic, from the clash between cars and pedestrians, from the need to provide new buildings for rising populations and expanding business districts. By leaving all this on the ground and allowing a completely new, and above all adaptable, cityscape above, the Clusters in the Air promised to remedy these problems. They would make cities more dynamic, and more amenable to the rapid social and economic change of the late twentieth century.

Each Cluster needed only a small amount of ground area. This made Clusters in the Air especially suitable in Japan, where land is at a premium because of the way most of the cities are jammed into the narrow band between the mountainous central area and the coast.

Buildings such as this constituted a revolutionary leap, yet even these unprecedented giants had structural roots in traditional architecture. The way the branches are cantilevered out from the cores, extending only a small distance on the lower floors, but gradually getting longer at higher levels, recalls something on a much smaller scale – the wooden brackets holding up roofs in ancient Japanese temples.

These brackets step out, getting gradually wider, and support a roof that tapers in the opposite direction, producing a balanced effect that works structurally and is visually harmonious. Isozaki created a similar balance in the way in which the Clusters are arranged.

The Clusters in the Air project represented a brave attempt to redefine the city – to declutter it, to make it adaptable and to economize on land. It did not go the whole way, using the megastructures to contain every kind of urban function, from flats to factories, but it did suggest a new way of looking at urban design. As change continued to accelerate into the twenty-first century, projects such as the Clusters in the Air still have something to tell us about how cities need to build to adapt.

WALKING CITY

Ron Herron, 1964

The Robotic City That Could Wander the Earth and Go Where It Is Needed

Between 1964 and 1966, the world of architecture was introduced to the Walking City, a concept for a metropolis consisting of a series of mobile structures that could move about on enormous telescopic steel legs. The idea seemed to come from the world of science fiction, and to owe more to the art of drawing and collage than to what people usually see as architecture. Yet the creator of the Walking City was

By depicting the Walking City against a backdrop of Manhattan, Herron stressed the contrast between his project's mobile, low-slung, animal-like qualities and the static, vertical, land-bound nature of the classic American city.

Ron Herron, an architect who, as he puts it, 'attempts to make architecture by fusing building, technology, and art to make something "special" for the user'.

Herron was a member of Archigram, a group of British architects that proposed numerous far-out schemes in the 1960s and 1970s. The members of Archigram – Warren Chalk, Peter Cook, Dennis Crompton, David Greene, Ron Herron and Michael Webb – did not earn their livings by getting things built. They were and are important for their ideas and their influence, which they spread through exhibitions, pamphlets, lectures, teaching and a kind of multimedia show called the *Archigram Opera*. They were very good at publicity – Peter Cook even got himself photographed (with Twiggy, Tom Courtney and Joe Orton) for *Queen* magazine.

Their most famous projects – all unbuilt – included the Plug-In City (a framework into which standard dwellings could be fitted), the Living Pod (a movable dwelling), the Instant City (an airborne city that could arrive where it was needed, hovering above the ground suspended from balloons) and the Walking City. These were designs that stood on its head the idea that architecture was about creating fixed, permanent structures. They embraced technology. They accepted consumerism and the idea of disposal commodities. They looked beyond the conventions of building to produce structures that could resemble machines or organic growths.

The Walking City consists of multi-storey buildings mounted on legs – the most famous drawing shows structures that seem to be at least thirty storeys high. The ambulant buildings mostly have an ovoid, rather insect-like form. The city is designed to be movable so that it can shift to another site if the existing one proves unsuitable, or so that it can go where it is needed. If it looks like something out of science fiction, this is because the drawings prepared by Herron bristle with technological detail. But they tell the viewer little about how the structures were meant to work in practice.

These great walking forms are very much of their time. They seem to draw their inspiration in part from military technology. One possible source is the Second World War Maunsell forts – steel, anti-aircraft forts moored to the riverbed in the Thames estuary and supported on tall, metal legs. These were in the news in the mid-1960s because in 1964 a pirate radio station had started to transmit from one of the forts, having added a long scaffolding pole (on which flew the skull and crossbones flag) as an antenna. The structures of the Walking City reminded some people of the forts, and Herron's architecture was criticized by some as war-like. At a conference in Folkestone in 1966, Herron was heckled with shouts of 'fascism', 'war machine' and 'totalitarian' when he spoke about the Walking City.

Herron may have been interested in the appearance of the Maunsell forts, but he was no fascist. For Archigram and its supporters, the metallic forms of the city were more like survival pods than weapons, structures that could protect people in the face of a disaster – nuclear war being the most pressing such fear in 1964. The city might be needed anywhere: a wilderness or a conventional metropolis. Herron's drawing shows the Walking City striding towards New York

City, knee-deep in the water of the Hudson River, with the Manhattan skyline behind. The image conveys its designer's daring, not only to have the pods walking through water, but also to juxtapose it with one of the great cities of the world.

There was something jokey about this coming together of opposites – solid, permanent New York and the shifting, water-borne Walking City. This hint of humour was emphasized by Archigram's visual style, which drew on collages using magazine imagery, space-age typography and Day-Glo colours. But there was also a serious point: that it would be useful to rethink the city, and that technology might have solutions to the world's problems. This, too, was an idea very much of its time – shifting a city around on insectile legs was going to require a huge amount of fuel, and the design could only come from a period when consumption was not the issue it is now.

So if they were unbuilt, unbuildable and impractical, why are Archigram's designs so important? First, because they make people look at things differently. Like Richard Buckminster Fuller's ideas (see Dome over Manhattan entry on page 220), they overturn existing notions and ask difficult questions (as Fuller asked: 'How much does your building weigh?'). If you question orthodoxies about buildings being permanent, heavy, rectilinear objects, that questioning might lead to new and promising paths.

Some architects certainly thought so. When Richard Rogers and Renzo Piano designed the Pompidou Centre in Paris – with its eccentric exterior, all coloured ducts, pipes and escalator-carrying tubes, and its adaptable interior spaces – they were influenced by Archigram. Other architects who have been given the label High-tech at some point in their careers, such as Norman Foster and Nicholas Grimshaw (whose work has celebrated the way a building is constructed or has used grid-like structures to which prefabricated modular elements have been added), are working in the same area as Archigram. And the team influenced thousands of architects through their teaching. Concepts such as prefabrication, lightweight structures and adaptability were not invented by Archigram. But their questioning, their provocative graphics and their flair for publicity brought such ideas into the public eye, and made it possible to entertain, seriously for a while, the notion that a city could walk through water and plug itself into the infrastructure of Manhattan.

OVERLEAF *One of the units that make up the Walking City illustrates the radical rethinking of architecture that Archigram proposed. Modern life may mean that, although we need shelter, this will not necessarily be provided by what we think of as 'houses' or 'buildings'.*

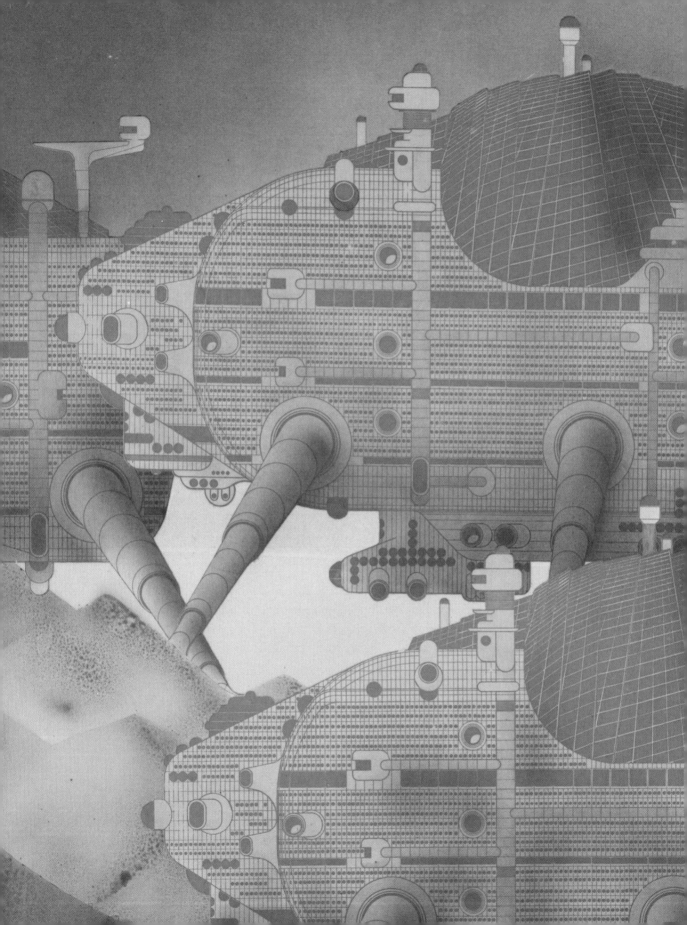

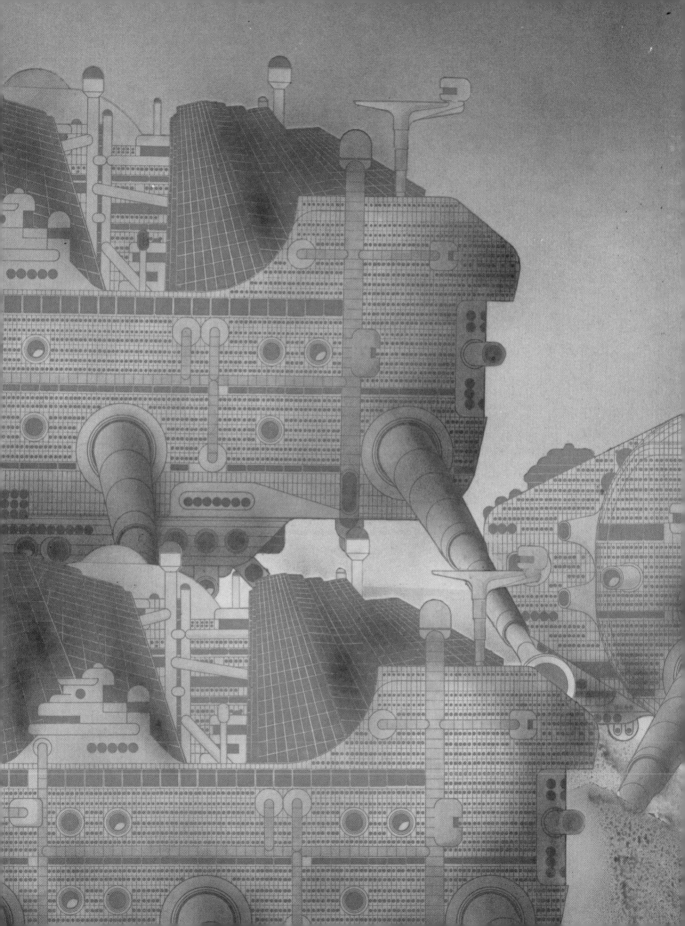

JERSEY CORRIDOR

Peter Eisenman and Michael Graves, 1965

A City in the Form of a Megastructure Nearly Fifty Miles Long

On Christmas Eve 1965, *Life* magazine published a special double issue on the American city. The tone was set on the cover, with the heading 'The U.S. City: Its Greatness is at Stake'. This was both a celebration of the vibrant cities of the USA and a look at how they might rise to the major challenges they were facing. The celebration came in features such as a photo essay on the shining surfaces and sheer stylishness of New York City. The challenges took various forms, from ineffective planning ('no-one's in charge', 'L.A. just said the hell with it') to slum dwellings, traffic levels and pollution. The magazine looked at ways that cities were destroying themselves and their surroundings (poor conversions of buildings or low-quality ribbon developments snaking their way across the countryside) and at how city planners were improving things (Boston's regeneration, Pittsburgh's efforts to rid itself of the scars caused by industrial pollution). Finally, *Life* magazine presented the future, in the form of various proposals for new cities and new city developments. One such scheme was by the Japanese master Kenzo Tange with his Tokyo Bay Plan (see entry on page 194). Another was a project designed by two then little-known young American architects, both professors at Princeton University, Peter Eisenman and Michael Graves. In the *Life* article, the pair were not credited: the scheme was attributed simply to 'a team of Princeton University professors'.

Both architects were later to become leading figures in very different ways: Graves as a pioneer Postmodernist; Eisenman as a master of Deconstructivist architecture. However, their city project is not obviously related to their later work. Called the Jersey Corridor, it is a conurbation in the form of a Modernist megastructure, a vast elongated complex designed to stretch the 47 miles (76km) from South Amboy to Trenton, New Jersey, and to contain every function – workplaces, housing, shops, leisure facilities, services – that one would expect to find in a city. The structure, referred to as a linear city, was to be built along a highway in two parallel bands

OPPOSITE *The Jersey Corridor scheme separates functions while keeping them physically close. Covered parking areas and roads occupy the lower levels while there is space for pedestrians to walk or gather in the open air above. Housing is provided in the tall buildings to the left; workplaces are to the right, connected by bridges but separated by physical space.*

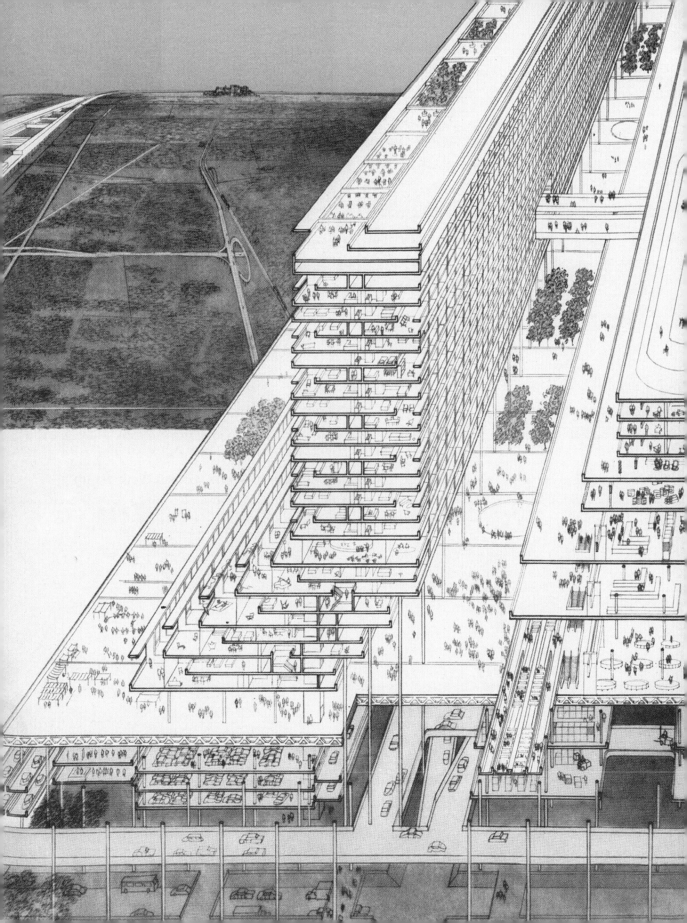

– one containing apartments, offices and local shops, the other light industry and larger shops, with linking bridges housing community facilities; roads run beneath them. The strips were multi-storey, so, although broad, left plenty of room for unspoiled countryside to stretch from their walls far into the distance. The idea of a linear city was not new. The influential Spanish urban planner Antonio Soria y Mata drew up a linear plan for the city of Madrid in the nineteenth century, and the concept had also been taken up by Soviet Russian planners in the early twentieth century. But the new take on it provided by Eisenman and Graves was in tune with 1960s' preoccupations and needs – road transport and high-density building were accommodated together.

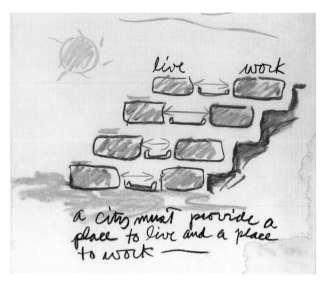

The architects produced simple sketches to sum up basic principles. Here the proximity of spaces for living and working is the key point.

Graves and Eisenman illustrated their proposal with a set of ink and pastel drawings: one showing an overall view of the complex, its two bands stretching into the distance; and another in more detail, cut away at the ends to produce a cross-section and give some idea of the structure (concrete floors supported on a grid of columns) and of the arrangement of functions. The 'downtown strip' – the part containing everything from housing to shops – is revealed in two separate parts: a tall section with about twenty-five above-ground floors, mainly devoted to apartments; and a shorter part containing mostly shops and other businesses.

Beneath sit several underground layers, accommodating mainly car parking and highways, through roads at the very bottom and local access routes above them. There are electric-powered vehicles, which residents can summon to their door, to make short-range travel easy, but the idea was to keep travel within the city to a minimum, by placing apartments close to shops and offices. By including countless tiny figures in the cutaway drawing, the architects gave some human scale to this vast structure – although in a sense this is counter-productive: one online reaction to the frenetic human activity in the drawings saw the result as something like a vast anthill.

The architecture revealed in the drawings in *Life* is Modernist. Eisenman and Graves rejected attempts at the creation of a pseudo-vernacular city, with low-rise houses built in some traditional American style, perhaps arranged on curving suburban streets. They also eschewed the cliff-like Brutalist architecture then fashionable, in which raw concrete was in evidence everywhere and buildings often had a rock-like, angular look. Their version of

This sketch emphasizes the importance of growth and change. The structure is built alongside a transport artery and can expand to the other side of the track when the need arises.

Modernism was more influenced by the style of Le Corbusier (see Ville Radieuse entry on page 162), in which tall buildings were expressed as a series of flat planes held up on pillars or pilotis. One model for the layout was probably Le Corbusier's Unités d'habitation – concrete blocks containing a mix of multi-level flats, shops and other facilities – which had been built in cities such as Marseilles. Le Corbusier used raw concrete in the Unités; the structures in the Eisenman and Graves drawing have a smoother, white-walled finish, but on a huge scale.

The Jersey Corridor was indeed conceived as an enormous structure, but Eisenman and Graves suggested that it could actually grow into something even larger. More and more linear cities could be added, until the entire North American continent could be crossed by a connected linear megacity, leaving much of the rest of the undeveloped land pristine or free for farming. As it was, the Jersey Corridor would have been the largest structure on Earth.

It was not, of course, built. It was, after all, a project by a group of academics, thoughtfully designed, buildable, but done without the backing or investment needed to give such a scheme a chance of becoming reality. However, the proposal was well known for a while because it appeared in a major, mass-circulation magazine. Few other architects' designs enjoyed such publicity, with the chance of reaching a large, non-specialist audience. Its very exposure in this way helped to encourage public awareness of new ways of thinking about city planning. Excited by its difference, its daring, its sheer size, the Jersey Corridor must have seemed, for a while, to many Americans, like the future.

NATIONAL SHRINE

Philip Johnson, 1966

A Memorial to Honour the People Who Immigrated to the USA

Ellis Island, in Upper New York Bay, housed the buildings where people immigrating to the USA between 1892 and 1954 were processed on entering the country. Originally housed in wooden buildings, the immigration station was rebuilt again *c.*1900 after a fire. The facilities were expanded to keep pace with the increasing numbers of arrivals, and the island itself was enlarged by reclaiming land from the bay. The big main building, built in the French Renaissance style in 1900, was still functioning when the immigration station closed. By that time, some 16 million men, women and children had passed through Ellis Island on their way to a new life in the USA.

When the immigration station closed in November 1954 the buildings were left empty and gradually deteriorated. Around ten years later, the government decided to do something about the site to preserve its dignity and create a memorial on the island. In May 1965, President Lyndon B. Johnson signed the legislation that made Ellis Island a national monument. Shortly afterwards, the American architect Philip Johnson was commissioned to produce a plan for a memorial and museum to honour the millions who had passed through Ellis Island in the sixty-two years that it was in operation.

Philip Johnson was one of the most prominent US architects. As a young man he was among those who introduced European Modernist architecture to North America. He had been one of the organizers of an epoch-making exhibition held at New York's Museum of Modern Art (MoMA) in 1932, which presented to the USA the work of such key figures as Walter Gropius, Le Corbusier and Mies van der Rohe. After Mies moved to the USA in the late 1930s, Johnson helped him establish himself there, and worked with him on such important projects as the Seagram Building in New York. And, by the 1960s, Johnson had designed various major buildings in his own right, such as his own residence, the transparent Glass House at New Canaan, Connecticut, which was famous all over the world.

Johnson knew that Ellis Island would be a sensitive project – everyone, from politicians to immigrants, popular journalists to specialist critics, would have an opinion about what to do with the site. The job seemed to ask for a major building, but there were decaying historical structures on the island and the Statue of Liberty was not far away. The architect would have to tread carefully in order to respect the opinions of others while producing a design that did not overwhelm the existing buildings or the famous statue.

Johnson's plan has two main parts. First, he made a radical and to many surprising proposal for the existing buildings on the island. He decided to leave these structures as managed ruins. They were already starting to fall apart, so the architect suggested removing the roofs, glazing and wooden fittings, and stabilizing the walls that were left. This would create, Johnson argued, an atmospheric and dignified space in which visitors could quietly contemplate the countless people who had passed through.

Secondly, he proposed a completely new structure for the site, a large memorial to the 16 million immigrants. His design takes the form of a circular structure, open at the top, with walls sloping inwards – in other words, a truncated cone. The

Johnson's monument is dominated by the exterior spiral ramp, which gives interest to the building's form while providing access to visitors, who would be able to read the names of countless immigrants to the USA.

The Immigration Station was
built c.1900 in a then-fashionable
Renaissance Revival style. It has
since been restored to house an
immigration museum.

surface of the cone is punctuated with vertical ribs, and the
whole structure is 300ft (91m) in diameter and 130ft (40m)
high – a tactful 20ft (6m) shorter than the pedestal of the Statue
of Liberty, which was clearly visible on Liberty Island, about
1700ft (518m) from the site.

Helical ramps wind around the cone, on both the inside
and outside. Also attached to the structure is a succession of
plaques, on which are inscribed all the known names of the
people who had passed through the immigration station.
The plaques are placed so that visitors would be able to read
the names from the ramp. It was suggested that this should
be done by reproducing the original shipping manifests,
so bringing an element of historical immediacy to the
otherwise very modern-looking memorial. The structure is
thus an impressively large memorial that pays tribute to the
immigrants as individuals while attempting to keep a low
profile in the context of the site and Liberty herself.

When the plans were unveiled they were endorsed by the
Secretary of the Interior Stewart Udall and by New York
Senator Jacob Javits. However, many people did not see the
virtues of tact or respect in Johnson's scheme. Press reports
dubbed the memorial ugly; people started to refer to it as
Johnson's Tower of Babel. The *Herald Tribune* compared
the design to 'a monstrous gas tank'. In an editorial, the *New
York Times* saw Johnson's monument as a wall, and pointed
out that walls normally keep people apart, so were a totally
inappropriate symbol for Ellis Island, which was a gateway
to America.

The press also took exception to the way the plans turned
the existing historic buildings into ruins. The ruination of the
buildings was seen as disrespectful and fake. Commentators

could find none of the romantic attachment to ruins often felt by European writers – perhaps because the architect had proposed taking an active hand in removing parts of the structures. The *World Telegram and Sun* described the idea as 'romanticism run riot'. A few writers took a kinder view – the renowned architectural critic Ada Louise Huxtable (writing in the *New York Times*) was more admiring, for example, and more appreciative of the memorial's originality. But the general reaction was unfavourable.

It was not simply these responses that scuppered Johnson's scheme for Ellis Island. In the middle of the Vietnam War, the government found it hard to afford the plans. A sum of $6 million had been earmarked for the scheme, but Johnson's design looked likely to cost much more than that. In the event, Congress did not even draw on the $6 million, and the plans were dropped on financial grounds. The historic buildings on Ellis Island, meanwhile, were left to decay in their own time, without professional architectural help.

The island had to wait more than fifteen years for a new set of plans. The 1980s saw Ellis Island's renovation linked with a scheme to restore the Statue of Liberty, but the new proposal for the island involved the building of a commercial hotel and conference centre. Many people – including the influential businessman Lee Iacocca, who was a government adviser and head of fundraising for the Statue of Liberty restoration – thought this idea too commercial and just as disrespectful as the Johnson plan, and it was dropped, in turn. Eventually, the main building on Ellis Island was adapted to house an immigration museum.

Johnson's scheme is now a footnote in the career of a major architect, and is little known to the general public. But it has importance as a brave attempt to memorialize the people who passed through Ellis Island. It also looked forward to a very different memorial – one also using a list of names on a wall – that America has now embraced. The Vietnam Veterans Memorial in Washington DC contains the Vietnam Veterans Memorial Wall designed by Maya Lin and completed in 1982. This bears the names of 58,315 dead servicemen and women, and is one of the most successful and worthy of all war memorials. There is some poetic justice in the fact that it remembers those who died in the very war whose funding effectively put a stop to Johnson's less graceful truncated cone on Ellis Island.

DOME OVER MANHATTAN

Richard Buckminster Fuller, 1968

The Ultimate Dome, Covering Part of New York City in a Diaphanous Skin

The 1960s was not only an era of optimism, youth culture, pop, hippies and new technology, but also a challenging time when Europe was still trying to rebuild after the Second World War and the USA faced social issues such as housing shortages. Could new technologies offer solutions to some of these problems? Some people such as American engineer and designer Richard Buckminster Fuller thought that they could. Bucky Fuller, as he was widely known, was a master at coming up with ingenious, left-field solutions to contemporary problems: for example, a streamlined car with a body like an aircraft fuselage; a circular factory-produced house that could be erected at speed; and a 'living package' containing all the furniture and utensils you would need for your house. Most of these ideas were too far-out (or, as Fuller's friends said, too ahead of their time) to catch on. But they were nothing compared with his biggest idea of all – his 1960s' plan to build a vast, 2 mile- (3.2km-) wide dome covering most of midtown Manhattan.

Fuller was fascinated by domes and their structural properties and advantages. A dome can enclose a very large volume with a minimum of materials. The walls of a dome can be relatively thin but still strong, just as a sheet of paper gets stronger when rolled into a cylindrical shape. If the walls of a dome are very thin, then it takes less steel or concrete to build, and this keeps the cost down.

Fuller realized that one particular kind of dome magnified these advantages. This was the geodesic dome, a structure strengthened by a rigid framework of straight lines. The classic geodesic dome is a curved form made up of many triangular surfaces. A framework of tubes or rods forms the sides of the triangles – this can be made of steel, aluminium tubing or wood. The triangles are filled in with some flat material – it could be sheet metal, glass, plastic or plywood. The result is a structure that is very light in weight and relatively strong.

The geodesic dome was not Fuller's idea – it had been invented by Walther Bauersfeld in Germany in the early 1920s.

OVERLEAF *Fuller's 2 mile- (3.2km-) diameter dome was designed to roof a swathe of midtown Manhattan, and to be high enough to cover the 103-storey Empire State Building.*

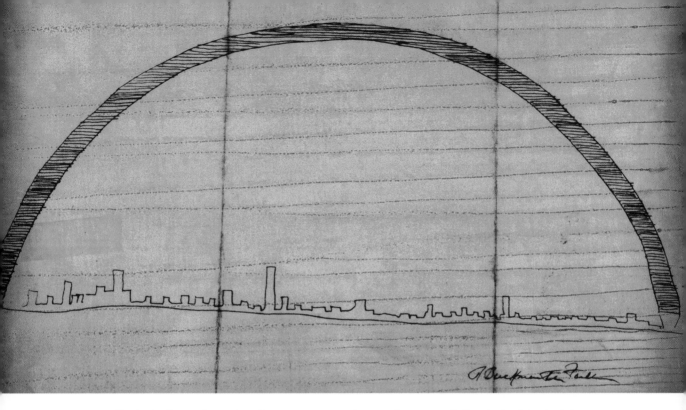

Fuller latched onto the notion about twenty years later, and patented it in the USA. As geodesic domes are inexpensive in relation to the volume they contain and are not difficult to construct, he saw them as a cheap way of addressing the post-war housing shortage. For various reasons this didn't work out (for one thing, most people don't want to live in round houses), but in the 1950s and 1960s domes found roles fulfilling all kinds of needs, from exhibition buildings to concert halls, storage facilities to defence early-warning systems.

By the 1960s, Fuller was designing really large domes, and discovered in the process that the bigger the dome the bigger the savings of materials and cost. So he started to speculate about whether it might be possible to build a whole city under a gigantic curving shelter – or even to erect a dome over an existing city such as New York.

Looking at a map of Manhattan in *c*.1960, he saw that at 42nd Street the island was about 2 miles (3.2km) across. What would be the effect of constructing a dome 2 miles (3.2km) in diameter over this part of New York City, stretching from the East River to the Hudson, and from 21st to 64th Street? Working with his architectural partner Shoji Sandao, he calculated that the surface area of such a dome would be around one-eightieth of the surface area of the New York buildings that it sheltered. Buildings leak heat through their

Fuller calculated that the shell of a large geodesic dome would require a substantial framework, indicated by the shaded area in this drawing. He even considered the possibility of using this space to house habitable structures.

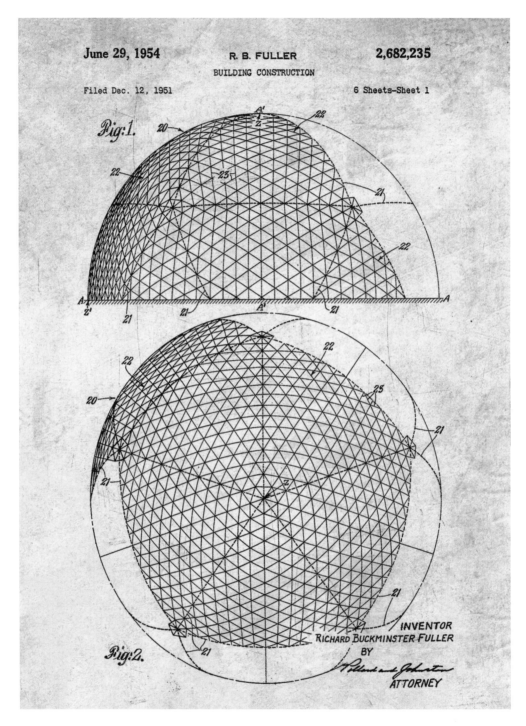

June 29, 1954   R. B. FULLER   2,682,235

BUILDING CONSTRUCTION

Filed Dec. 12, 1951   6 Sheets-Sheet 1

Fig:1.

Fig:2.

INVENTOR
RICHARD BUCKMINSTER FULLER
BY
ATTORNEY

walls, windows and roofs, so by reducing so dramatically the surface area that was exposed to the elements the dome could cut heat loss to a tiny fraction of what it had been. There would be vast energy savings, as well as a reliable, comfortable interior climate.

The US patent taken out by Fuller indicates the framework was made up of equilateral triangles.

Fuller and Sandao knew that the chances of building their dome over Manhattan were minimal. It was not so much the scale of the project that daunted Fuller – he worked out that you could pay for the dome in ten years with the money you saved on snow clearance. The vested interests of the various owners of land and buildings, the arguments between supporters and objectors, the politics – these would be the factors that would make such a project impossible.

Fuller did not work out exactly how the dome would be built. He did, though, suggest that the covering could be wire-reinforced, shatterproof glass, and that this could be mist-plated with aluminium so that glare would be cut down without cutting out the light. From the outside, the surface would be like a vast, glinting mirror. The environment inside would be pleasant. As Fuller says of another geodesic dome: 'From the inside, there will be uninterrupted visual contact with the exterior world. The sun and moon will shine in the landscape, and the sky will be completely visible, but the unpleasant effects of climate, heat, dust, bugs, glare, etc. will be modulated by the skin to provide a Garden of Eden interior.'

With the mirror-like surface in mind, Fuller presented his idea using an aerial photograph of New York, with the dome painted over it using an airbrush. The effect is totally bizarre – a structure with no visible means of support, and so diaphanous that it looks as if it could puncture, like a balloon. Perhaps this did not do the idea any favours – it's easy to dismiss this image as hare-brained. And yet, like so many of its inventor's ideas, it was based on reasonable arguments and assumptions.

Other potential advantages of a structure such as this, although unlikely to be felt in Manhattan, might be useful elsewhere. In places with a rainy season, most of the rain disappears into storm drains – the precious water is never used and cannot be stored for the dry season when water is short. With a dome, a system could be built to take away the rain and store it in a reservoir. The climate-control possibilities even meant that it might be able to use huge domes to accommodate people in the Arctic and Antarctic. Such bold and ambitious schemes never came to fruition. But big geodesic domes on exhibition sites and in industrial parks remain, as does scientists' name for a carbon molecule with a geodesic structure – Buckminsterfullerene – to remind us of Fuller's influence, on both large and microscopic scales.

THE PEAK

Dame Zaha Hadid, 1982–3

An Artificial 'Granite Mountain' Standing Out Above the Congestion of Hong Kong

The Iraqi-born British architect Dame Zaha Hadid died in 2016 with one of the best and most high-profile reputations in her profession. She was the first woman to win the Pritzker Architecture Prize in America and to be awarded the Gold Medal of the Royal Institute of British Architects (RIBA) in the UK. She had completed prestigious buildings – such as important museums, university buildings and the aquatics centre for the London Olympics – all over the world. Her architecture, with its distinctive but ever-changing curvaceous geometry, stood out and led one newspaper to call her 'the queen of the curve'. Yet her success was slow in coming and she worked for a number of years without getting anything built.

When Hadid first began to be noticed in the early 1980s, her abilities as a painter stood out as much as her designs. She was especially engaged by the work of the Russian Suprematist artists of the early twentieth century, particularly Kazimir Malevich. Malevich used basic geometric shapes – circles, squares, rectangles – in abstract compositions, usually with quite a restricted colour palette. Some of his images such as the celebrated Black Square are very simple compositions with a single shape, while others arrange a number of shapes, apparently suspended in space, to produce very dynamic results. Hadid took to painting buildings and cities in a similar way, reducing their forms to simple geometry. Anyone interested in early twentieth-century art will see another element in her paintings – one related to Cubism – with subjects so angled that the viewer feels able to see everything at once. Add to all this the very fluid feel of the images – paint, itself liquid and flowing, is not the architect's usual medium – and you get a very individual blend.

The results were stunning works in their own right, but they aimed to do more than stun the viewer: 'I was very fascinated by abstraction and how it really could lead to abstracting plans, moving away from certain dogmas about what architecture is.' Hadid used painting to explore and

portray all kinds of projects, from large-scale city plans to individual buildings, and the project for which she first became well known involved paintings both of the building itself and its dramatic city setting.

This project was a building in Hong Kong called The Peak. Hadid did the design as an entry for a competition for an upmarket leisure club also containing apartments. Her design's starting point is the site and what the architect called its 'Suprematist geology'. This comprises not just the rocks on which the city was built but also the 'built geology' of tower blocks and lower-rise structures that are crammed onto Hong Kong's tightly constrained site. Hadid's paintings of Hong Kong reflect this, with the crystalline forms of skyscrapers crowded between sea and mountain, all delineated in shades of blue, pink and grey.

The leisure club was designed to overlook the city, and here the architect's engagement with the geology became clear. She

Zaha Hadid's painting of The Peak depicts the building in the context of the city, which is seen as urban geology, where buildings and mountains merge.

proposed excavating part of the site and then using the rock that had been removed to build an artificial cliff. The club was to be built on this cliff, resulting in a breaking down of the distinction between site and building.

But if architecture and site seem to merge together, the building itself is very different from the architecture of the rest of Hong Kong. It consists of a series of horizontal elements, looking rather like enlarged beams, some containing apartments, some parts of the club. Other parts of the structure, including a snack bar and a swimming pool, are dramatically suspended in a void between two of the beams.

The drama of the building comes from the way the beams seem to be suspended in the air, with the parts like the pool held between them in turn. The plan is made still more spectacular because it is not based on a Modernist grid. Upper layers are set at an acute angle to the ones beneath, to give the structure a daring, precarious quality. Whereas Modernist architecture was centred on the right angle, Hadid's here seems to be all about diagonals. Some parts of the building are curved, carrying the rejection of the grid still farther. Flowing curves were increasingly to be a feature of Hadid's architecture, combining with the diagonals and giving her structures a feeling of movement. This was a very distinctive kind of architecture from the mainstream. It seemed deliberately designed to stand out, and to be different – but always with a functional reason for the difference from the buildings around it.

It was a convincing formula: Hadid's design won first prize in the competition. However, The Peak was not built. Perhaps it seemed too daring. But it was still in many ways the architect's breakthrough design and had the chance to make an impact when it was shown in a major exhibition, Deconstructivist Architecture, at New York's Museum of Modern Art (MoMA) in 1988. This exhibition showed how architects in the 1980s were challenging the role of the old Modernist geometry, with its ubiquitous right angles. In this new world of zigzags, diagonals and curves, The Peak naturally shone.

Hadid's plans and paintings were infectiously engaging, drawing viewers in to explore the forms and their relationship to their setting. At the same time they established their creator as an innovative designer, offering a very clear vision and one that transformed its visual sources in Suprematist art into something that was both three-dimensional and new.

A site drawing shows the overlapping levels of The Peak in the context of the local geography and existing buildings.

It was a long time before Hadid was able to turn one of her daring architectural projects into the reality of a finished building. This came some ten years later, with structures such as the Vitra Fire Station in Weil am Rhein, Germany. By this time, though, her reputation was already established because of the way in which projects such as The Peak had captured the hearts and minds of the architectural profession, her name already well known before any concrete had been poured or bricks laid.

TOUR SANS FINS

Jean Nouvel, 1992

A Tower That Fades into the Sky and Disappears into the Ground

The idea of the building as a landmark is as old as architecture, but it gained extra traction in the late twentieth century, as developers and governments began to realize what architects had always known – that a single building can transform a whole city or district, can become its image or symbolize its 'brand'. France's President François Mitterrand grasped this idea when he conceived his series of 'Grands Projets', the big building projects or modern monuments that were instigated in Paris during his time in power, and that raised the city's profile, architecturally and culturally. The success and fame of these government-backed public buildings reminded commercial builders and property developers that they, too, could create what came to be called 'icons'.

Paris's large La Défense business district is home to many commercial developments. It began to take its present form in the late 1950s, when offices started to replace the open spaces, factories and other structures on the site. These early developments were not very tall – there was a height limit of 330ft (100m) – but they were well positioned, just west of the city and on the historical axis formed by the city's two great triumphal arches, the Arc de Triomphe at the Étoile and the Arc de Triomphe du Carrousel. The district expanded in the period from the 1970s to the early 1990s, with further waves of office buildings; at this stage, the height restriction was dropped and these new offices took the form of ever-taller towers. By 1982, it was clear that La Défense was one of the world's major commercial areas, and it soon had a monument to complete the historical axis. This was the Grande Arche de la Défense, which was one of President Mitterrand's Grands Projets. It combines a square arch form with office buildings for the government in the sides and an exhibition centre in the upper section.

The Grande Arche was in a part of the district that had still not been fully built over. There was, for example, a small triangle of vacant land nearby, between railway tracks and so

ripe for development. A competition was held for a building for the site, and the winner was Jean Nouvel, an architect already well known for his outstanding Institut du Monde Arabe, another of the Grands Projets. Nouvel's plan was for a circular tower, designed to be among the world's tallest buildings, at 1394ft (425m) high, and one of its narrowest, at just 143ft (44m) in diameter. It was a design of unusual poise and grace.

The tower's odd name – Tour Sans Fins means 'tower without ends' – embodies its unique design. Nouvel's idea was

In contrast to the solid, four-square form of the nearby Grande Arche de la Défense, the Tour Sans Fins merges with the surrounding shadows at the base, while blending with the clouds at the top, thereby reducing the effect of the building's great height.

to make the top of the tower fade into the sky and the base of the building melt into the ground, so that it is apparently endless. He does this by sinking the base into a pit or crater, and cladding the building's lower storeys in unpolished black granite, so that they appear to disappear into the earth. Above the black granite section, various materials are used for the building's outer skin, and these get gradually lighter at the higher levels – black granite, anthracite granite, polished mica, aluminium, stainless steel. The windows use various types of reflective and clear glass, ending with transparent glass at the top, so that the building seems to merge with the sky.

Structurally, the Tour Sans Fins is unusual for its time. The typical skyscraper of the period had a concrete core that provided most of the structural strength, with the floors cantilevered out like tree branches and a thin, non-structural skin of glass or another cladding material. Nouvel's tower has its structure on the outside, a framework of concrete with huge glass windows. This leaves most of the internal floors free for office space, which is arranged in three vertical stacks, each of twenty-four storeys, with lobbies in between.

One of the structural problems facing anyone planning a tall building is wind load. Tall towers move a surprising amount in the wind – the top of a tall building can sway as much as 3ft (1m). As well as ensuring the structure can withstand the effects of the wind, architects and engineers have to reduce the movement because it can be upsetting – and nausea-inducing – for those inside. Although the wind load on a slender circular tower is less than its rectangular equivalent, a tower of this height (1394ft/425m) still poses a challenge for the engineers. Nouvel worked on the design with an engineering team from renowned practice Ove Arup, led by Tony Fitzpatrick. They specified a device called a tuned mass damper to compensate for the wind load. This is a large and heavy weight that is installed at the top of a tower and is designed to move from side to side when the building starts to be affected by the wind, effectively reducing the vibrations and removing the risk of nausea for those inside.

So structurally the Tour Sans Fins was carefully planned and visually it is stunning. The amount of attention (and potentially the amount of money) that was devoted to its appearance was typical of Nouvel, but unusual in a commercial building project such as the Tour Sans Fins, which was intended to be funded by private investment. It was, though,

highly appropriate for a prominent site such as the one at
La Défense, and for a building that would be visible across
Paris. Unfortunately, the need for private funding was the
main stumbling block to the project's progress. The history
of La Défense had been one of stops and starts as the French
economy swung between boom and slump. In the 1990s,
another downturn put the project on hold and eventually led
to its abandonment.

Looking across Paris westwards towards La Défense now
reveals a large cluster of towers. But there is none of the focus
that a tall and elegant building such as Nouvel's might have
given them. There is another loss – a wider one to architecture.
If it had been built, the Tour Sans Fins would have given
developers a lesson in restraint. Nouvel's tower works as a
design because it is subtle, and shows how a tall building,
usually the most assertive kind of structure there can be, can
work in a more understated way, and one that pays respect to
the earth and the sky. More recent tall buildings tend to make
their mark by adopting some unusual shape or form that
makes them stand out much less subtly. Developers could
learn more from Nouvel's rethink of the way a skyscraper
can occupy its site.

*Nouvel's model places the Tour
Sans Fins in the context of its
restricted triangular site, hemmed
in by the surrounding buildings.*

BANGKOK HYPERBUILDING

Rem Koolhaas, 1996

A Bundle of Towers, Diagonals and Horizontals, Linked by Elevators and Cable Cars

The name may be new but the concept is ancient. A hyperbuilding is simply a very large structure that can house a huge number of people and contain many different functions within its walls. Perhaps the Tower of Babel was the first hyperbuilding, but twenty- and twenty-first-century mixed-use towers such as Chicago's John Hancock Center or Dubai's Burj Khalifa, which accommodate apartments, hotels, shops, restaurants, galleries and car parks, also have some claim to the name.

Diagonal boulevards span the adjacent water, giving access to different parts of the Bangkok Hyperbuilding at various levels.

The work of the Dutch architect Rem Koolhaas has been shaking up the built environment for several decades now. Koolhaas and his practice OMA as well as its spin-off group AMO have had a particular impact on thinking about city architecture and planning, through buildings, publications and unbuilt projects – some of them very large. Dynamic, bold and huge, the hyperbuilding OMA proposed for the city of Bangkok is one of the most dramatic – a structure that looks from some angles as if a number of conventional buildings have been literally 'shaken up' and left as a questioning collection of verticals and diagonals. Yet there is thought and logic behind this apparent confusion.

Various principles underlie the Bangkok Hyperbuilding. One is a familiar idea in planning around tall buildings: that urban sprawl – the bane of modern cities – can be avoided if you build tall structures that leave room for greenery. With the hyperbuilding, where you can house 120,000 people and the services and even workplaces that they require, there is a far greater chance of reducing sprawl and increasing the amount of green space. The building needs only 3 per cent of the space required to house the same number in a conventional development. Another key principle is reducing the distance between home and workplace, cutting down on travel time and energy consumption.

Koolhaas has pointed out that in many ways this kind of structure is more fitting for a city in a newly developing area, where the shock of rapid expansion and the arrival of modern facilities can wreak havoc on existing urban spaces. The hyperbuilding would supply the sudden, growing need for a new city, fitted for contemporary needs, without enveloping precious rural land, as conventional ad hoc urban sprawl would do.

Bangkok, a city with a long history and one that has been growing and modernizing rapidly over the last few decades, is a rather different case. Koolhaas has described it as 'a city on the edge of the tolerable', in which traffic, disorganized development and volatile politics make it hard to create spaces in which it is easy to live and work. There is still a pressing need for new accommodation and facilities, and to reduce the relentless urban sprawl. A hyperbuilding could, argues Koolhaas, supply such a demand, but involves specific challenges such as siting in relation to the existing city, links to it and balancing of facilities with what is already there.

The designers see the hyperbuilding as a city or city quarter, and its parts are analogous with the parts of a conventional city. As the architects put it: 'To achieve urban variety and complexity, the building is structured as a metaphor of the city: towers constitute streets, horizontal elements are parks, volumes are districts, and diagonals are boulevards.'

In Bangkok, the idea was to site the hyperbuilding near the edge of an already existing business district, so that its inhabitants could work either there or in the megastructure itself. The proposed location was in a green reserve, near the Chao Phraya river – and in part straddling the river to give access to the rest of the city. This site was an undeveloped area that would leave green space around most of the building. Moving through a hyperbuilding, and making connections with the outside world, are crucial. In the Bangkok Hyperbuilding, there are several ways of moving around: vertical elevators connecting the building's different levels; horizontal 'boulevards' equipped with cable cars and 'gondolas' linking it to the ground and the existing city; and a 'walkable promenade'.

The structure is unusual. A cluster of towers is linked at various levels by broad, planar horizontals and tied to the ground by the four diagonal 'boulevards'. This cluster-like arrangement means that the building 'reads' as several buildings in one, something that sets this hyperbuilding apart from the typical mixed-use towers seen in the world's major cities. Yet, although this unusual structure looks complex at first glance, it was intended to be relatively simple. The Bangkok Hyperbuilding is not an essay in high technology. Its various elements – towers, planes, diagonals – are similar to the most basic of architectural parts: pillars, beams and struts.

It is designed on an enormous scale. A model set next to a miniature of the Eiffel Tower shows that the tallest part of the structure is about four times as high – and far higher than the much more low-rise buildings of Bangkok in the neighbouring district. However, the way in which the building is fragmented into several towers makes it less monumental than it would be if its whole community of 120,000 could be crammed into a single, monolithic building such as a twentieth-century Tower of Babel. This is in keeping with Koolhaas's principle that when a building becomes very large it is no longer satisfactory to create it with a single architectural gesture – the structure therefore needs to be fragmented. So while it seems perverse

OPPOSITE *Looking down on the model shows how the structure occupies undeveloped land while also adding its own green spaces, high above the ground. The diagonal boulevards (INSET) reach into the heart of the structure.*

to use the term 'lightness' in relation to such a vast structure, the relatively slender elements have a delicacy about them that is unexpected. Their proportions and arrangement would also make them light and airy inside.

Its unusual configuration makes the hyperbuilding a standout project for Koolhaas and OMA, even though it is unbuilt. It is also important because it points towards a less monolithic way of answering the need for more urban buildings, and because it integrates architecture with city planning in a new kind of structure. Hyperbuildings such as this might not begin to sprout on the edges of the world's big cities in the foreseeable future, but they show that a megastructure does not have to be a monolithic lump, and can have transparency, lightness and grace.

SHENZHEN, CHINA

ASIAN CAIRNS

Vincent Callebaut, 2013

Vertical 'Farmscrapers' Designed to Transform a Chinese City

As long as there have been architects, we have looked to them to offer a better future. From the ideal cities of the Renaissance to the new start promised by the Enlightenment, from the urban expansion of the nineteenth century to the technological dreams of the twentieth, architects have offered solutions to urban problems and suggested new ways to live. We have not always followed their lead – ideals can be impractical. But their work has offered a fund of ideas, and has sometimes provided hints about the future.

Today, the fastest-changing place on the planet – the place with the greatest need for an urban rethink – is probably China. This country is facing a seismic population movement to its cities. In 1980, about one-fifth of Chinese people lived in towns; now it is more than half, and still rising. There will soon be more than 220 cities with over 1 million inhabitants in China, and more than twenty with over 5 million. As a result, Chinese cities have been transformed architecturally: Shanghai is now a forest of skyscrapers. Shenzhen, once a market town of about 30,000 people, is now a megalopolis with an estimated population of 18 million. With increases such as these come all the familiar problems – high energy consumption, carbon emissions, food shortages and overcrowding. Cities consume 75 per cent of the Earth's energy and are responsible for 80 per cent of its carbon emissions. The need for architects to rise to these challenges is greater than ever.

There are many ways for architects to try to address these issues. Terms such as 'green architecture', 'eco-architecture' and 'sustainable architecture' have been used to describe a range of approaches that have tried to build such important features as waste recycling, low energy consumption, integration of building and green space, and reduction of carbon emissions, into everything from small houses to office blocks. Many of these designs are resolutely low-tech, using traditional materials (often local ones to bring down the carbon footprint) along with modern renewable energy technologies.

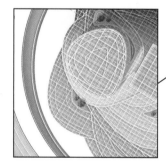

OPPOSITE *The six cairns are arranged symmetrically on a circular site. Each has a square tower at its core, which supports the layers of rounded structures, one above the other* (INSET).

What is happening in emerging and rapidly developing parts of the world such as China, however, seems to many people to demand a more radical approach.

Asian Cairns (2013) is the response of the Belgian architect Vincent Callebaut to these problems as experienced in the vast city of Shenzhen. This project brings the rural and the urban together in a tall structure: the garden tower or farmscraper. Visually, it is based on a cairn – the pile of pebbles left by a traveller by the wayside. Callebaut's project for Shenzhen brings together six of these farmscrapers on a circular site. Each structure is based on a tall, rectilinear tower. To this are attached a multitude of large, pebble-shaped structures that can accommodate a wide range of functions: housing, offices, manufacturing, leisure and, most importantly, food production. These pebble-shaped modules spiral around the central towers, which form both the structural support and the vertical boulevard or highway for the whole building. The pebbles can be clad in glass or solar panels, have wind turbines attached to them or have open tops to accommodate green spaces with trees.

High-tech as they look, the Asian Cairns take their cue from nature. Nature relies mainly on solar energy. It keeps waste down, using only the energy it needs. It recycles constantly. It fosters biodiversity. Callebaut uses all these principles in his design. He also draws formally on shapes seen in the natural world: curvaceous pebbles, spiralling nautilus shells, structures that combine toughness with plasticity (he refers both to the flexibility of lily pads and the resilience of bees' nests in writing about the project). So both the appearance and the process involved draw heavily on the natural world.

Many of the effects of bringing so many functions together in the farmscrapers are similar to the goals of the other megastructures proposed by architects over the decades: for example, the reduction of commuting and the consequent cut in energy consumption and pollution; the creation of a whole community in one densely packed location; and the economies of scale. But the Asian Cairns add to the mix. The structures are designed to incorporate the recycling of waste, to produce as much of their own energy as possible and to contribute to the oxygenation of the city through planting. By including organic agriculture, they cut down on our use of artificial chemicals in food production, promote food autonomy and contribute to the biodiversity of the city. Moving more food production to the city would also help the rural environment by reducing the need to resort to deforestation.

Asian Cairns is structurally exciting, visually spectacular and holistic in approach. It is not unique in these qualities – Callebaut is not the only architect to suggest incorporating farming into a tall, urban building – but it is remarkably integrated and engagingly biomorphic. Yet perhaps the most interesting thing about the project is that it attempts to turn the old view of architecture upside down. Historically, architecture has been seen as protecting humans from the forces of nature, as shutting out wind, rain and snow, as keeping out the cold of winter or shading us from the heat of the summer sun. Asian Cairns is trying to work *with* nature, to reconcile humanity and the environment, in the hope that this will lead to a more sustainable way of living.

Vernacular architecture, the catch-all term for the traditional ways of building using local materials (and managing without architects) all over the world, has always worked with nature, responding to specific local climate conditions, social conventions and agriculture. Vernacular architecture is generally low-tech, homespun, low-rise and simple. Structures such as Asian Cairns, on the other hand, throw at the building everything technology can offer, from steel beams to photovoltaic panels, in the hope that harmony between the human race and the rest of the natural world will result. China's expanding cities present a challenge of an unprecedented size, and may need solutions on this kind of scale. So long as architects keep rising to this challenge, there is some hope for the future.

OVERLEAF *Callebaut conceived the Asian Cairns as organic structures, rising out of a forest setting and adding to the greenery with their own aerial vegetation and farms.*